AF560862

REFLECTIONS ON INDIAN ENGLISH FICTION

Edited by
M.R. VERMA
A.K. SHARMA

Published by

B-2, Vishal Enclave, Opp. Rajouri Garden,
New Delhi-110027
Phones : 25413460, 25429987, 25466842

Sales Office
7/22, Ansari Road, Darya Ganj,
New Delhi–110002
Phones : 23273880, 23275880, 23280451
Fax : 91-11-23285873
web : www.atlanticbooks.com
e-mail : info@atlanticbooks.com

ISBN 81-269-0410-0

Printed in India
at Nice Printing Press, Delhi

PREFACE

If today Indian English literature has acquired recognition and respect in English-speaking world, the credit for it largely goes to Indian English fiction. Indian English novel has shown amazing growth during the last seven decades or so. Unlike Indian English poetry which took a long time in outgrowing the imitative stage or Indian English drama which never really took off, Indian English novel has shown a variety of themes as well as a maturity in narrative skill since the mid-1930s when the Big Trio of the Indian English Novel—Mulk Raj Anand, R.K. Narayan and Raja Rao—appeared on the scene. By 1960s novelists like Anita Desai and Arun Joshi were exploring the complex inner world of modern Indians. By 1980s, with novelists like Vikram Seth and Arundhati Roy, Indian English novel made the English-speaking world sit up and take notice of it. International awards that had trickled so far began to flow more frequently. Of late women novelists like Shoba De, Shashi Deshpande and Manju Kapur have added a feministic touch to the depiction of Indian life and sensibility. With the growth of Indian English novel critical studies on them have also grown in volume and approaches. The area, however, is so rich that a constant endeavour in this regard is needed. The present book is an attempt with the same view in mind.

The book presents a collection of essays that are wide ranging not only in the choice of authors—two of the Big Trio, R.K. Narayan and Raja Rao, on the one hand, and the recent ones like Upamanyu Chatterjee and Manju Kapur on the other—but also in the different angles from which these novelists have been discussed. It includes a much talked about author like Arundhati Roy as well as a remarkable but less discussed writer like Ruskin Bond. It consists of feminist studies as well as semiotic study and post-modern reading. We hope that the book will interest the lovers of Indian English novel.

–M.R. Verma
A.K. Sharma

CONTENTS

1

V.S. NAIPAULS *A BEND IN THE RIVER*: A CRITICAL STUDY

ASHOK KUMAR BACHCHAN

In *A Bend In The River,* V.S. Naipaul records his impressions of Africa and its inhabitants confronting an ethnic problem of displacement. It is a disturbing novel in which the smouldering fire of violence caused by acute frustration and anger finds a memorable expression. Naipaul gathered material for this novel during his visit to Zaire in 1965. He published an article in the New York Review of Books which provides much insight into *A Bend In The River:*

> To Joseph Conrad, Stanley Ville—in 1890 the Stanley Falls station—was the heart of darkness.... Seventy years later at this bend in the river something like Conrad's fantasy came to pass.[1]

Naipaul has discussed in the article how the original inhabitants of Africa lost their identity not because of encounter with forces of nature but ironically because of their contact with the forces of civilization established by the Europeans. In an interview with Hardwick, Naipaul records his feelings about the humiliations suffered by the Africans in the new set-up in these words:

> The Africans were camping in the houses just the way the ancient English centred in the abandoned villas of the Romans.[2]

V.S. Naipaul has brilliantly presented the setting in *A Bend In The River* in the following lines:

> The place had had its troubles: the town at the bend in the river was more than half destroyed. What had been the European suburb near the rapids had been burnt down, and bush had grown over the ruins, it was hard to distinguish what had been gardens from what had been streets.[3]

The setting resembles Congo or Zaire of the sixties to a certain extent. In part the political set-up reminds one of the African country described by Naipaul in an earlier novel, *In A Free State.* The revolution is over and the country is now ruled by a mysterious adventurer called the Big Man who is invested, in popular imagination, with both omniscience and omnipotence. The President holds the country in his grip by his rhetoric, guile, sorcery and of course, brute force. The landscape is barren, blighted and desolate symbolizing the chaotic state of affairs and indicating violence: 'Too many of the places on the way have closed down or are full of blood' (9).

In *A Bend In The River,* the landscape is veiled in mysterious darkness. Naipaul, like Conrad, exhibits his skill of adding tension to the story through an evocative description of the dark and inaccessible terrain. The landscape extends into the heart of Africa. Like other novels, *A Bend In The River* has a reporter as a character. Salim is a young and sensitive man of Indian origin, lonely and displaced in his surroundings. He is compelled to leave his family and settle in an up-country town. He confesses that he did not belong to the place and his family came from the coast, which is not truly African. He remarks:

> Many miles of scrub or desert separated us from the up-country people: he looked east to the lands with which we traded—Arabia, India, Persia—These were also the lands of our ancestors. But we could no longer say that we were Arabians or Indians or Persians, when we compared ourselves with these people, we felt like people of Africa (17).

Salim remarks with nostalgia, an uneasy feeling about his alienation from native Africans, in these words:

> It was an Arab Indian—Persians—Portuguese place, and we who lived there were really people of the Indian Ocean. True Africa was at our back (17).

Salim realizes that his life in Africa is quite unstable and insecure, even though he has achieved commercial success. He recalls:

> We had the occasional comfort of reward, but in good times or bad we lived with the knowledge that we were expendable, that our labour might at any moment go to waste, that we ourselves might be smashed up; and that others would replace us (94).

Salim, thus, shares the fate of every uprooted tribe and, to a certain extent, he shares the fate of other natives who also constantly live in fear of being up-rooted because of the recurrent tribal clashes. Naipaul observes:

> To an African, a child of the forest, who had marched down hundreds of miles from the interior and was far from his village and tribe, the protection of a foreign family was preferable to being alone among strange and unfriendly Africans (19).

In spite of all these troubles Salim looks for a fresh start when his family base on the coast is threatened. The events, which compelled him to start a new life in the heart of the continent, however, do not turn out to be propitious or rewarding as believed by him in the beginning. Naipaul suggests very imaginatively through the description of the setting itself that Salim's effort is bound to fail. This kind of foreboding, a sense of doom, was also expressed in Naipaul's *Guerrillas*, where Meredith had sounded the alarm: 'The setting may change but no one will make a fresh start or do anything new.'[4] Naipaul describes the site chosen by Salim for his fresh venture. Salim, of course, becomes the chief spokesman of the novelist. There are also three other voices who provide their own impressions and sustain narrative interests of the novel. They even enrich Salim's observation by adding to it or sometimes detracting from it. Salim is the most acute observer and at times his comments become confessional. He continues to explore something new even realizing that this attractive place is actually a death-trap. The vivid description of the site with its water-hyacinth surrounding the water is a suggestive image. Hyacinth is repeated quite a number of times, thereby acquiring a symbolical significance:

> The tall lilac flower had appeared only a few years before, and in the local language there was no word for it. The people still called it 'the new thing' or 'the new thing in the river' and to them it was another enemy. Its rubbery vines and leaves formed thick tangles of vegetation that adhered to the river banks and clogged up waterways. It grew fast, faster than men could destroy it with the tools they had. The channels to the villages had to be constantly cleared. Night and day, the water-hyacinth floated up from the south, seeding itself as it travelled (51).

In spite of its beauty the lilac-coloured flowers stand for death and destruction and the image also symbolizes rootlessness apart from its damaging function of choking waterways. The narrator of the novel, Salim drifts and floats through the surge of social and political changes like the self-seeding water hyacinth. Prof. Nondita Mason regards Salim as 'the dominant consciousness of the novel.'[5]

Salim recapitulates and senses frustration but at the same time he also accepts the bitter truth of colonial history. However, this does not stop him from asking the painful question at a crucial moment:

> But where was the good place? I could not say. I never thought constructively about it. I was waiting for some illumination to come to me, to guide me to the good place and the 'life;' I was still waiting for (102-3).

Indar, the son of a wealthy coastal money lender, shares the pain of exile like Salim but his fate is a bit different because he has his British University degree to fall back upon. Thus, Indar is a man of two worlds and that accounts paradoxically for his survival as a citizen of the world. He seems to be telling Salim the secret of his success in the midst of flux and drift. He fails to secure a job in England and even the Indian High Commission refuses to employ him because of his divided loyalty Thus, Indar has no choice but to serve in Africa and he tries to get the approval of the President with his new ideas of progress. Indar, once again, comes back to London, the place which he has rejected once out of a feeling of insecurity. A Few critics have found fault with Indar's portrayal as to them Indar appears to be play-acting and does not appear to be a person fighting for survival. Indar is a deluded man Naipaul tries to be protective towards him for that very reason.

Nazaruddin is another exiled man who shares the same family background. His daughter is betrothed to Salim. He is quite different from Indar. He is a survivor and, in spite of his taste for good things of life, has a genuine resilience and in-built capacity to bounce back. He even anticipates the future troubles and manages everything in a shrewd manner. He tells Salim:

> You must always know when to pull out. A businessman is a mathematician. Remember that, never become hypnotized by the beauty of numbers. A businessman is someone who buys at ten and is happy to get out at twelve (29).

Nazaruddin is essentially a man of our times and is perhaps Naipaul's nearest success to create a contemporary man. Naipaul regretted to a reviewer that contemporary writers have not been able to write about the interest of a particular period:

> One must capture the interest of this period. I don't believe the world has at all been written about. The world is no new.[6]

Nazaruddin's perception about the Arabs, Asians, Europeans and Americans is acutely relevant and unflattering in the novel. Naipaul's world is not an imaginary one, it is frighteningly real. John Leonard has rightly emphasized Naipaul's strength as a novelist:

> Unlike Sal Bellow or John Updike or Graham Greene or Joseph Conrad, Mr Naipaul has not invented an Africa. He doesn't need an imaginative construction to dazzle himself or the reader into sentience. He reports and thinks and feels, and the field, the domain is suddenly full of vectors. The future is a ruin not yet achieved, 'no family, no flag, no fetish' and no place to hide.[7]

Mahesh, an Indian trader in Africa, is another exile in the novel. Mahesh spends his blessed days along with his beautiful wife, Shoba. His whole effort is directed in asking his family life a bulwark against the assault of history. Naipaul observes succinctly:

> Like many isolated people, they were wrapped up in themselves and not too interested in the world outside (34).

Salim, the novelist's mouthpiece, is however, unimpressed and he feels that Mahesh lacks Nazaruddin's world view. Mahesh is certainly a small merchant with his grim determination to carry on. Mahesh may be regarded as a survivor from a limited point of view because he pulls off a coup and even gets the Big-burger franchise. Still his survival was related to his casual outlook. In spite of his casual manner, Mahesh can't conceal his bitterness and at least once he remarks without any reservation: 'It is not that there's no right and wrong here. There is no right' (99). These different viewpoints on the state of affairs in Africa combine to present a somewhat cohesive, though mainly negative view of the expatriates in Africa. In his political novels, Naipaul appears to be nearer to Balzac and Conrad in his avoidance of sentimentalism and absolute fidelity to experience. His clear sightedness is obvious in his portrayal of small characters like Zabeth, Raymond, Yvette, Ferdinand, Metty and Father Huisman. Though Naipaul sometimes appears to be suffering from certain inbuilt prejudices, yet he is certainly free from the more serious failing, that is the bane of sentimentality. Zabeth, in her physical description, appears at least from an outsider's view, a large exotic African woman from the dark interiors. However, Naipaul resists the temptation to treat her as a noble savage. He does not idealize her character, but all the same, she is presented as a woman of tremendous vitality and what is more, essential sanity. This becomes clear when she warns Salim against the machination of the President:

> He is killing those men, Salim. They are screaming inside and he knows they're screaming. And you know Salim that is not a fetish, he's got there (232).

Metty whose name is a derivative of the French word which means a mixed race, has enough sanity and like Zabeth, he can see through the game of deception handled by the ruler. He has escaped from the coast after a bloody riot in which the Africans and Muslims are badly involved. Naipaul brings out the brutality of people involved in this senseless killing: 'They were behaving, as though knives did not cut as though people weren't made of flesh' (37). Naipaul denounces the motiveless malignity of people once again in his description of the murder of father Huisman, a missionary and true lover of Africa. Metty and Ferdinand, the latter being Zabeth's son, are meant for satiric exposures as both of them ape the manners of the colonial masters and try to imitate their skill and life style conveniently ignoring their own native resources and moorings. Naipaul's comment is pertinent:

> This better life lay outside the timeless ways of village and river. It lay in education and the acquiring of new skills; and for Zebeth, as for many Africans of her generation, education was something only foreigners could give (41).

Both Ferdinand and Metty spend their days in the town by indulging in wine and women. Naipaul presents the degradation of the colonial victims who suffer from crisis of values and even their western education does not ensure their future but leaves them more insecure in the end. Naipaul's comment is expressed through Salim in this manner:

> Now I felt his affectations were more than affectations, that his personality had become fluid. I began to feel that there was nothing there, and the thought of a lycée full of Ferdinands made me nervous (53).

Ferdinand's trip to America also results into a failure. Ultimately Ferdinand comes back to Africa and joins the polytechnic at the Domain, a place which attracts many foreigners and European teachers. He ends up his career by becoming a Commissioner. It is the Domain which invites people like Indar, Raymond and, of course, Yvette at the bend of the river. All these three persons finally share the same fate, but Naipaul's treatment varies. His portraiture of Raymond is fairly severe and he shows him to be a deadwood scholar who has 'made Africa his subject because he had come to Africa and because he was a scholar used to working with papers, and had found this place full of new papers' (187).

Raymond in his fifties and his young wife, Yvette share a marital discord and join the ranks of Bobby and Linda and they become the third European couple in exile to be treated by Naipaul. Yvette's background before her arrival in Africa recalls Jane's. Like her she was also poor and ambitious and Raymond almost dazzled and seduced her by spending more money on dinner one evening than her father earned in a week. Thus Africa seems to be the land of her dreams for leading a glamorous life with balls and dinners at the President's mansion. She enjoys these privileges until Raymond falls out of grace with the President. At this juncture like Jane again, she begins to fret and fume and realizes her mistake. Like the women-protagonists of the preceding political novels, Yvette resorts to mindless sex to escape the boredom and frustration of reality. As usual, Salim's sexual involvement with Yvette has been presented in a very cold-blooded, almost clinical manner. Salim has no illusion either when he is involved with Yvette and confesses:

> My wish for an adventure with Yvette was a wish to be taken upto the skies, to be removed from the life I had—the dullness, the pointless tension, 'the situation of the country.' It wasn't a wish to be involved with people as trapped as myself (191).

Yvette parallels Jane in her sexual greed. The culminating scene between Salim and Yvette is almost similar as the one presented in *Guerrillas* between Jimmy and Jane. Salim is less violent than Jimmy and he does not kill her, but his behavior is no less shocking. His contempt is clearly pronounced in his typical reactions:

> At this moment I held her legs apart. She raised them slightly smooth concavities of flesh on either side of the inner ridge—and then I spat on her between the legs until I had no more spit (227).

The breakdown of Yvette and Salim's relationship is not at all unnatural because theirs was a temporary liaison born out of a need to fill their vacant and almost meaningless lives. Like previous novels, there are shades of homosexual relationship between Salim and Metty and this has been imaginatively suggested.

The marital life of Mahesh and Shoba, the beautiful Indian couple, does not seem to flower into ideal relationship. Mahesh remains ignoble and half a man. Naipaul tries to account for the failure of the power of love in terms of the broader disintegration of social forces. His characters appear to be passive, numb and self-absorbed. Sometimes they look like puppets being acted upon by some other forces, while at other times they seem to be overacting. Even the President, Big Man, perhaps modelled upon Henry J. Taylor's protagonist, remains in the background and we are made aware of the fact through the casual remarks of the novelist and characters that he is also handled by certain big power.

Naipaul's acute detachment from his characters is quite remarkable in *A Bend In The River*. He does not side with the white or with the black. The officers are little better than their European counterparts and Naipaul comments about them:

> With their guns and jeeps, these men were poacher of ivory and thieves of gold. Ivory gold—add slaves, and it would have been like being back in oldest Africa. And these men would have dealt in slaves, if there was still a market (99).

Naipaul's treatment of the whole scene in the modern Africa has something to do with his travel book, *Loss of El Dorado,* where he speaks of the extinction of Chaguana's Indians by the Spanish conquerers and in *A Bend In The River* he presents a parallel situation and convincingly demonstrates that neither colonisers nor liberated savages alone have a monopoly on cruelty.

The structure of *A Bend In The River* reminds us of *Guerrillas*. There are three zones of action—the town at the bend in the river where Salim runs his dry goods' shop, the Domain, an artificial enclave built for the big Man's White men, and lastly, the capital, the pretentious home of the Big

Man. Naipaul starts by presenting a beautiful description of the place where Salim arrives with new hopes:

> In the daylight—though the colours could be very pale and ghostly, with the heat mist at times suggesting a colder climate—you could imagine the town being rebuilt and spreading. You could imagine the forests being uprooted, the roads being laid across cracks and swamps (14).

Naipaul, then, moves to the Domain, an artificial region, with the people who are equally artificial. The place is full of cracks and flaws. He has pictured the scene both realistically and symbolically:

> The building of the Domain had run up fast, and the flaws that lamplight had hidden were noticeable in the midday brightness. The plaster on the walls had cracked in many places, and in one place the cracks followed the stepped pattern of the hollow clay bricks below.... The windows were open; with no protecting roof, no trees outside, just the levelled land, the room was full of light and glare, and there was no feeling of shelter (176).

The description brings out the artificiality of the place as well as the unnatural presence of the dwellers like Raymond and Yvette who have reached there to heal their souls and finally realized that it is no blessing for them. Salim rightly notes that in spite of Raymond's boasting of high connections the latter is a defeated man and his home is a house of death.

The capital, the third zone of action, the place is deliberately shrouded in mystery just as the Big Man, the modern version of Kurtz. The novelist does not present the Big Man visually and only once the glimpse of his habitat is presented. Salim describes the city:

> The city, while decaying in the centre, with dirty roads and rubbish mounds just at the back of the great colonial boulevards, was yet full of new public works. Large areas near the river had been turned into Presidential reserves—palaces with great walls, gardens, state-houses of various sorts (259).

In other words, the capital is a strange place with unusual combination of dirty roads, rubbish mound and colonial boulevards. The place also presents the image of the big Man as Salim rightly feels at a certain moment that the President is bypassing the real Africa in his frenzy to radicalize the country. His failure is suggested beautifully through the imagery of water hyacinths which end their journey in the capital itself.

The climax of the novel shows that neither of the characters is destined to last and each one is bound to face a debacle. Even Salim finally meets with humiliation. In order to remove his boredom Salim makes a trip to London to see Nazaruddin, his prospective father-in-law. But even London provides just a temporary relief. Naipaul has presented brilliantly the theme of rootlessness as the common destiny of the contemporary man. Salim comments:

> In the streets of London I saw these people, who were like myself, as from a distance. I saw the young girls selling packets of cigarettes at midnight, seemingly imprisoned in their kiosks, like puppets in a puppet theatre. They were cut off from the life of the great city where they had come to live and I wondered about the pointlessness of their own hard life, the pointlessness of their difficult journey (238).

Salim is engaged to Kareisha, Nazaruddin's daughter, who settles herself as a Pharmacist in London. Nazaruddin himself comes to London after experiencing bitter tastes of life in Canada and Uganda. He is also cheated in London by the Algerians as he was previously betrayed in Canada. Hence Nazaruddin generalizes like every embittered man, his experiences of the world: 'We've come here (London) at the wrong time. But never mind. It's the wrong time everywhere else too' (247). But Europe is not the last of Salim's disappointments as his homecoming also results into a disaster. His store has been snatched and given to a citizen Theotime. Salim is accused of smuggling and thrown into jail, but he is rescued by the new commissioner, Ferdinand, the son of Zabeth.

Salim leaves Africa for the last time on the river-boat and he notices some positive symptoms of violence in the air around:

> After the morning heat it had turned stormy, and in the silver-storm light the overgrown, bushy bank was brilliant green against the black sky. Below this brilliant green the earth was bright red. The wind blew, and ruffled away reflections from the river surface near the bank. But the rain that followed didn't last long, we sailed out of it (286).

The bright colours mentioned in these lines refer to the possibility of explosion and a search light on the river shows a boat full of Africans and other natives who look like flying insects trying to escape both the bush and water hyacinths. Naipaul, in an interview with Hardwick remarked that the encroaching bush embodies 'the breakdown of institutions of the contract between man and man. It is theft, corruption, racist incitement.'[8]

It is obvious that in *A Bend In the River,* Naipaul presents a documentary account of the turbulent Africa undergoing drastic changes through war and killings. In such a situation the sensitive individuals who stand for dignity and sanity can have nothing but complete isolation. But even this isolation promises security and order which is the dream of all aspiring individuals. Hence Naipaul's characters finally hide in dark rooms while they have the whole world to move into and they turn inwards in self-defence.

Naipaul's political novels including *A Bend In The River* appear to be too cruel and tragic. The fact remains that they have not darkened or soured the author's compassion or his belief in the future of man. Naipaul simply demonstrates that such things have happened before and will happen again. Even if the future holds no promises of security, there is no room for nostalgia. Like Nazaruddin, Naipaul hints at the need of carrying on even in the midst of all confusion, chaos and violence.

NOTES AND REFERENCES

1. V.S. Naipaul, 'A New king for the Congo,' *New York Review Books* (26th June, 1975), 24.
2. Hardwick, 'Meeting V.S. Naipaul.' *New York Times,* 36.
3. V.S. Naipaul, *A Bend In The River* (Penguin), 10. (All other page references in parentheses are from this very edition).

4. V.S. Naipaul, *Guerrillas* (Penguin), 149.
5. Nondita Mason, *The Fiction of V.S. Naipaul* (The World Press, Calcutta, 1986), 106.
6. Mel Gussow, 'The Writer without Roots,' *New York Times*, (26 December, 1978), 22.
7. John Leonard, 'A Review of the Novel,' *New York Times* (14th May, 1979), 21.
8. Hardwick, *op. cit*, 36.

2

THE ELEMENT OF HUMAN COMPASSION IN THE NOVELS OF KAMALA MARKANDAYA

SARITA VERMA

One can't miss the presence of human compassion in the novels of Kamala Markandaya which lends the philosophic and religious charm to her writings. Though married to an Englishman and permanently settled in England, Markandaya's entire creative work is dedicated to India. Being well-acquainted with both the cultural backgrounds, one can't possibly overlook the encounters of East and West in her works which represent altogether different philosophies. Individuality of the man is of peak importance to the West while East thinks not of individual lives but of life, in which the individual is merely a part of the phenomena and considers that every living creature is an extension of the same pure light of the Divine Creator.

Both Eastern as well as Western characters of Markandaya advocate their own ideologies and religious beliefs to the point of being incomprehensible to the other. They identify with Rudyard kipling's idea:

You'll never plumb the oriental mind
And if you did it isn't worth the toil.[1]

No doubt her Western characters find the concepts of universal individualism, meekness and active charity quite incomprehensible but all her Indian characters strongly uphold the tradition of universal life and love by showing ample concern for animals, adhering to vegetarianism, providing shelter to destitute and deformed relatives etc. In all conflict with the evil, method to be used is love and not force, because in using evil methods to defeat evil, it is evil that wins. In a letter written to Margaret P. Joseph, Markandaya writes, "I detest cruelty to any living being."[2] This exactly is the innate philosophy of her life which finds its manifestation in loving descriptions of animals, the virtues of vegetarianism and respect for all life.

In *Nectar in a Sieve,* The protagonist Rukmani, on her way to her new home in her husband Nathan's cart, is glad to see the bullocks unyoked and led to the small pool of water near which they had stopped, "giving them each a handful of hay. After that rest the beasts began stepping, jauntily again."[3] The coming of the tannery to the village brings an upheaval in the fortunes of Rukmani and her husband Nathan. While going to the city in the cart to search for the son, Rukmani even in her tribulation is concerned over the bullock's sore:

> The animal is not well. I say to the man. He shrugs. What can I do? I have no other. I must make these trips since they are my livelihood.[4]

The cartman is forced to compromise his instincts of compassion and kindness for the sake of physical survival. Being a householder it is his sacred duty to look after his family also. Despite facing many vicissitudes, Rukmani is shown as a woman of courage and fortitude who gives a great specimen of her instinctive love, kindness and sacrificial nature, when she adopts the leper Puli, with whom she returns to her village after the death of her husband and whom she entrusts to Dr. Kenny's care.

Dr. Kenny is one of the few English characters, who is delineated by Markandaya as kind-hearted, sympathetic and compassionate. He is a philanthropist and great humanitarian. Out of his pity for the poverty-stricken and suffering people of India he has left his motherland, his wife and children and has come to stay among the people who are not his men and in a country which is not his own. He has in his heart a great solicitude for Indian people and love for their children. Though sometimes he gets disgusted with their follies, poverty and silent ungrudging humility. As is evidenced by his remark to Rukmani:

> I go when I am tired of your follies and stupidities, your external, shameful poverty. I can only take you people in small doses.[5]

Yet, his heart bleeds for them and always goes out to them in their sorrows and miseries. He has identified himself with the Indians so much that he does not feel himself an alien among them. Expressing his views before Rukmani he says:

> My country. Sometimes I do not know which is my country. Until today I had thought perhaps it was this.[6]

Kenny feels disturbed about ungrudging attitude of Indians over their misfortunes, he shouts:

> Why do you keep this ghastly silence? Why do you not demand—cry out for help—do something? There is nothing in this country. Oh God, there is nothing![7]

Rukmani tells him, We are taught to bear our sorrows in silence, and all this is so that the soul may be cleansed, he exclaims with disgust: My God! I do not understand you. I never will. Go, before I too am entangled in your philosophies.[8]

Through the depiction of these two characters, the novelist has shown the basic differences in the innate psyches of the Eastern as well as Western kindred souls.

In *Possession,* Valmiki growing up to become a famous painter in England under the patronage of Lady Caroline Bell, too, could not shake off his belief that "a part of God dwelt in every man and would one day reunite with the divine whole."[9] It lies at the root of his strict vegetarianism even in alienation. "Killing has no appeal for me, he says and Anasuya notices that despite his utterance there is no trace of the repugnance that would have been the old crude-reaction to what was in deep conflict not only with his inheritance of compassion but with the very nature of his religion."[10] British contact had blunted his prejudices but not his belief that *animals aren't created for men.* He perceives the death of his pet monkey Minou as punishment for the violation of this precept. Anasuya the Indian writer, holds a similar belief but she warns him that a lot of people do subscribe to the view that they are like the whole of Christendom. Valmiki firmly believes that animals are created in their own right and therefore feels that he must have stopped believing this when he bought the monkey, of which he took a possession like a god, for ends of his own.

Such compassion extends to his love for Ellie, the Jewish girl, ugly and scarred by the war and sick with its horrors. Valmiki loses part of his spiritualism when he decides to paint her in the nude to focus on her beauty. Yet when those paintings are lauded, he considers it blasphemy to exalt man-made over man. Caroline Bell by contrast is materialistic and possessive. She pays for Valmiki, brings him to England, pours care and money into nurturing his talent for her own ends, at the same time she also dissuades Annabel in advancing her relationship with Val, by revealing her, the circumstances of Ellie's unnatural death. Valmiki feels remorse for his doings and knows that death is only change.

Ravi, the Vagabond hero of *A Handful of Rice,* finds shelter from the police in Apu, the tailor's house. Despite his vices, Ravi is still in his primal state as far as philosophies are concerned. His love and compassion is reflected in his actions. He throws the plantain leaf on which *idlies* were served, to the cows nosing in the gutters. Apu's wife Jayamma too "had been brought up to respect every living being as the fragmentation of an eternal God."[11] When Ravi becomes rebellious and materialistic he loses his latent concern and love for living creatures. In a dejected mood, he kicks the stones in his path and when a dog prowls past sniffing the gutter, he picks up a jagged stone to throw at it but is held back by an urge, older and stronger. On the other hand, Apu has exemplified his universal love in supporting needy relatives and the cripple Kumaran even on his meagre resources. After Apu's death, Ravi commits incest with his mother-in-law. The reversal in his nature, his descent into gross crudities is because of his scant respect for life and love. They are seen as part of his urban influences deemed western-oriented and materialistic. No love can grow here so that Ravi's untainted love for Nalini grows sour. Though Ravi is not totally converted into Western pragmatism yet he is still hopeful of his rebirth but not in his present state.

In The Coffer Dams, the English technologists and Indian engineers close their ranks after the accident at the dam site when the lives of Indians and a few English are lost. When two Indian bodies are not traced the other labourers strike work. Rawlings, the short-tempered Englishman cannot understand the cause of fuss. But Clinton's wife Helen, who is on friendly terms with the Indians, reasons with her husband, "they believe the spirit will not be freed, until its body has been reverenced."[12]

Clinton fails to fathom the spirit behind such beliefs. Neither can Rawlings understand what Krishnan means by saying they will suffer spiritual torments, if the body is considered nothing when the spirit is gone. The body indeed is nothing, "it is the spirit that matters."[13] Krishnan asserts, but it is a matter of equal respect for their beliefs as the English wanted for their own. The English duly reverenced the body laying it in state till Doomsday and resurrection. To this end the English made sure the loam was freshly turned so that the dead could lie easy. The Indians preferring not to lie and moulder punctiliously observed funeral rites, burning the dead body and sending the ashes—as the English contemptuously thought—bowling merrily along on the river.

Helen has imbibed the spirit of understanding and love for innocent natives. Clinton wonders how she can get along with the natives, she tells him:

> I just think of them as human beings, that's all and further adds, "you've got to get beyond their skins, darling. It's a bit of hurdle, but it's an essential one."[14]

Finding her husband puzzled, she remarks jocularly:

> I expect it's something to do with being born in India in my previous life.[15]

Helen, the neutral observer in the novel realises that machines tend to make people callous inhuman and devoid of human values. She recedes from husband Clinton farther and farther each day because he perceives himself only as builder. For him steel and concrete are more important than human beings. Finding him indifferent to human misery, she asks him, "can't you care? Don't human beings matter anything to you? Do they have to be a special kind of flesh before they do?"[16]

Her bitter invective against modern European civilisation

finds its expression in her indignant outburst before tribal technician Bashiam:

> Our world. The one in which I live. Things are battered down in it under concrete and mortar, all sorts of things. The land. Our instincts. The people who work in our factories, they've forgotten what fresh air is like. Our animals—we would learn from them, but we are Christians you know, an arrogant people, so we deprive them of their rights. Deny them. Pretend they haven't got any. Then they don't know about sunshine or rain or either. Sometimes they can't move, poor things. We don't allow them to, in case they yield us ounce less of their flesh. Where is our instinct of pity? Blunted. We've cut ourselves off from our heritage. We've forgotten what we knew. Where can we turn to, to learn? A million years accumulating, and we know no better than to kick it in the teeth.[17]

It becomes clearly evident that Helen's love and compassion is not only confined to the human beings but it extends to the animals also. Often while wandering in the forest, she would embrace stray dogs, rub flea powder into their yellow coats. At night she would fondly observe the deer that came near her bungalow every night.

Gopal Rao is another kindred soul in this novel, who can not get over his non-violence. Vegetarianism has been part of his upbringing. He tries hard "not to think about those beefy men, the master builders who could stomach anything, flesh and blood and kidneys that reeked as he knew from watching them feed."[18] He squirms when he sees real flesh and blood at the accident site much to the chagrin of his friend Lefevre who like the other Englishman wonders why a dead body should be so repulsive to his friend for whom only the soul mattered.

In *The Nowhere Man,* Srinivas and his wife Vasantha, living in England for a long time, are still strictly vegetarian. After the death of his wife, Vasantha, Srinivas invites Mrs. Pickering to share his home but does not yield to her non-vegetarianism. His companionship with Mrs. Pickering is based on compassion. The turbulence and violence that follows the wake of racial agitation in England is detestable to him. It is alien to his spiritual make-up and he can not bear it. When Vasantha dies of tuberculosis in England he cremates her in the electric crematorium but as per his religious belief he carries a casket of her ashes for the immersion in the river. While spilling it in the Thames, he is scolded by the English policeman for polluting the beauty of the river but he pathetically explains that it was only his wife.

Srinivas's association with Mrs. Pickering brings in him an understanding of Christianity and he helps her to decorate a tree on Christmas to place by a window for the neighbours to see. He had been quite disinterested earlier, so this new gesture was well-approved by his neighbours who believed that at last he had become civilized.

In *Two Virgins,* Saroja and Lalitha grow up in the Hindu tradition and learn a respect for all living beings. They are of the firm belief that soul can't be destroyed though Lalitha has been explained by her teacher, Miss Mendoza that "Souls did not enter other bodies. They went straight upto heaven or down into hell or were cooped up in purgatory which was an in-between place for doing penance in"[19] till the day of resurrection when a bugle call awoke the dead. The animals had been created for man and God had given man domination over the beasts. But Lalitha was not convinced. Saroja feels concerned when Mannikam wants to sell a barren cow to the butcher. She feels relieved that his wife being a good Hindu would never agree for cow slaughter. Saroja watched as Mannikam's wife carefully batched the cow's udders and rubbed coconut fat into the splits. She was heard to say, "Should I grudge her mouthful of grass after all the milk has flowed from her these past years?"[20] Appa too was of the opinion that animals should never be grudged what men did not want.

Saroja's love flows unrestrained for all animals and she feels pity for the patient little ponies at he smithy's whose weary looks and the smell of their charred hoof made her distraught. These animals sometimes died in the shafts and drivers whose livelihood depended on them sometimes whipped them but passersby would get angry and restrain them.

Hindu philosophy enjoins that when man uses animals, he is not supposed to encroach its integrity and be circumspect. Markandaya makes this novel a spirited defence of her own Hindu beliefs and little else so that structurally the novel suffers—none of these defenses or invectives and diatribes against Christianity have any particular purpose. Amma is heard saying that Muslims and Europeans being flesh-eaters are callous of animal's feelings. But Markandaya soon corrects such a direct accusation with Lalitha declaring that Miss Mendoza had taught them that though flesh-eaters Europeans were kind to the animals, and with a later remark by Appa that like Muslims and Europeans, Hindu too could be equally callous about animals.

According to the interpretation of Hindu philosophy, the soul finds release only after its present embodiment of flesh and bones is fully destroyed on death. Appa's compatriot Rangu was cremated when he died in police action and his ashes were respectfully immersed in the river which absorbs both joys and sorrows because it is eternal, ever-flowing. *In The Golden Honey Comb,* once again, the destruction of life is averred by Indians. Indian villagers shake their fists at the two Europeans who have killed the birds. By introducing the tensions of such types, in her plots, Markandaya wants to acquaint the unknowing readers with the Indian philosophy.

It is evident from the above discussed novels that Kamala Markandaya has done full justice in delineating the kindred souls. It won't be wrong to say that the projection of such compassionate souls is her need to cling to her rich eastern heritage in alienation. Her adherence to the religious philosophy promises the release of soul from the pangs of rebirth and helps man to outgrow individualism and espouse the love and concern for all living creatures.

NOTES AND REFERENCES

1. Rudyard Kipling, *Departmental Ditties and Barrack Room Ballads,* 103.
2. Margaret P. Joseph, *Kamala Markandaya* (New Delhi: Arnold Heinemann, 1980), 214.
3. Kamala Markandaya, *Nectar in a Sieve* (Bombay: Jaico Publishing House, 1954), 3.

4. *Ibid.*, 140.
5. *Ibid.*, 71.
6. *Ibid.*, 109.
7. *Ibid.*, 43-44.
8. *Ibid.*, 114.
9. Kamala Markandaya, *Possession* (London: Putnam, 1963), 154.
10. *Ibid.*, 178.
11. Kamala Markandaya, *A Handful of Rice* (New Delhi: Orient Paperbacks, 1966), 55.
12. Kamala Markandaya, *The Coffer Dams* (Delhi: Hind, 1969), 177.
13. *Ibid.*, 179.
14. *Ibid.*, 12.
15. *Ibid.*, 12.
16. *Ibid.*, 105.
17. *Ibid.*, 138.
18. *Ibid.*, 171.
19. Kamala Markandaya, Two *Virgins* (Delhi: Vikas, 1974), 6.
20. *Ibid.*, 6.

3

VIKRAM SETH: *AN EQUAL MUSIC*

P.S. SANYAL

Of the recent practitioners of the Indian novel in English, published during the last two decades, the names of Salman Rushdie and Vikram Seth merit special attention. That Rushdie inaugurated a new kind of experimental fiction with an entirely different literary style has been recognized by perceptive readers, critics and new writers.[1] Earlier Makarand R. Paranjape, a contributor to a pioneering anthology of articles on the new novelists of 80s, had expressed his reaction thus:

"This momentous book really jolted the very foundation of Indian English novel. Its energy, its self-indulgence, irresponsibility, disorder and cockiness really shocked the day lights out of the staid form of the Indian English novel."[2] It is true that Rushdie popularized the 'new genre' in a good number of novels and created a vogue for employing the technique of 'Magic Realism.' Amitav Ghosh and Shashi Tharoor made a brilliant use of this device in their first novels like *The Circle of Reason* (1986) and *The Great Indian Novel* (1989) respectively. But like all fashions, Rushdie's fictional technique produced clones and created the impression of boredom and monotony where style and technique became an end in itself. In sharp contrast, Vikram Seth with his prodigious gifts added a new dimension to the Novel of Social Realism with his very first brilliant novel *The Golden Gate*, (1986). Though set in California, the novel in question was hailed as a thrilling literary event for reviving poetic novel against the background of every day experiences of the ordinary kind. However, in his next *A Suitable Boy* (1993), Vikram Seth wrote a truly Indian novel of epical dimensions. Though Seth claimed it to be a 'love story,' it documents the changes and various crises that the nation underwent in the wake of Independence, particularly in the Northern belt. Leaving aside the media hype, the novel's real contribution lay in 'restoring one's faith in the well-made novel or the fictional form.'[3] Like Jane Austen's novels, it can be viewed at once as a love story and critique of Indian democratic experiment.

As regards *An Equal Music* (1999), it at once confirms one's faith in Seth's creativity and competence. This novel is at once another bold experiment, and a new beginning. In a way it goes back to the milieu of the first novel for a change but now the characters are all European, though the novel is set entirely in the West. As one Indian reviewer has rightly observed, "It is a novel written with bone-bleached economy of expression and emotion."[4]

Certainly with this novel Vikram Seth presses his claim for inclusion in the company of those great modern fiction-writers who have combined beautifully a love story and love of music as part of their narratives.

In yet another sense, it makes a new beginning by establishing the value of love and culture in the midst of narrow sectarianism and cultural anarchy of modern "City states."

At first sight, the novel draws our attention by its 'epigraph,' which is an extract from a well-known sermon of John Donne. As the epigraph points out, it refers to a metaphysical state of being where there shall be "no cloud, nor sun, no darkness, no dazzling but one equal light, no noise, nor silence, but an equal music—one equal communion and identity."[5]

This obviously is a very tall order because such 'an equal music' refers to a sublime or transcendental experience. While there can be no denying that 'music is the 'food of love,' the fact remains that even a minimum deviation in terms of lack of concentration and repetitiveness and over elaboration can be a besetting sin which can elude the intended goal or objective. Centuries ago, Longinus, after locating the sources of sublimity, was frank enough to admit—"Excellence of style is the concomitant of a great soul."[6]

As a matter of fact, Vikram Seth, like Amit Choudhari, another promising practitioner of new Indian fiction, is also 'genuinely interested' in music. It is interesting to note that many novels of Amit Choudhuri have musical titles *viz.*, *A Strange and Sublime Address* (1991), *Afternoon Raga* (1993) and *Freedom Song* (1998). The critics have lavished adjectives like 'delicate,' 'lyrical,' 'evocative' in praise of this writer's works.

Similarly, Rushdie's latest novel *The Ground Beneath Her Feet* (1999) is also about the theme of love against the background of music, nay, 'rock music.' Rushdie himself is on record to have stated, "I would say above everything, it is a love story, a triangular love story. It has a huge social historical side but the thing which holds it together is the story of three people."[7]

Obviously, the novel of Rushdie deals with the group of Rock Singers whom the author had befriended over a long period.

While Rushdie's book presents a curious blurring of frontier or 'shadow lines' between the world of imagination and the real world, Vikram Seth's novel as usual, seeks to explore the complex relationships among a group of classical musicians. There is, however, a superficial similarity in the sense that Seth's novel acknowledges a new friendship and is dedicated to Philip Honore, a violinist, in verse.

While comparisons are inevitable, Seth is piqued by such attempts. As he observed, "I can not see why people are lumping the two of us together. Sure, we both wrote a book at the same time. But then, so do many other writers. Yes, we are both Indians but then Indians are one-fifth of humanity."[8]

Vikram Seth shows his awareness of superficial similarity—"Of course, we both wrote about music—Salman about Rock, I about classical music. We both wrote love—even more amazing co-incidence. But they are two different books."[9]

To begin with, *An Equal Music* (1999) is a novel of love and music set in the world of classical Western music. It moves from London to Vienna and Venice with an odd trip to Rochadale in the North of England. It traces the growth of love between two students of classical western music, which untimely ends in Vienna, the place where they had come in touch with each other as music students. The novel actually deals with "an odd quadripartite marriage with six relationships, any of which, at any given time could be cordial or neutral or strained."[10]

In fact, the main characters, apart from Julia and Michael, are Helen, her elder brother Piers and Billy, the narrator's father, his auntie Joan and Julia's husband, James Hansen, her friends Erica and Maria, the music teacher Prof. Carl Kall and the music critic Nicholas Spare and a pet cat Zsa—appear at regular intervals. Among the female characters, apart from Julia, Virginie, another music student, Helen and a lady Mrs. Formby play an important role in influencing the course of events and shaping the destiny of Michael Holmes.

The novel is divided into eight chapters but each chapter is sub-divided into several short scenes. However, there is no system or plan behind this arbitrary arrangement. The whole novel is presented through a hypersensitive eccentric, Michael who has a life-long obsession with or infatuation for Julia, even though she has moved out of his life following a misunderstanding. But the novel shows that even after her marriage, neither Julia nor Michael is prepared to forget the past and turn over a new leaf. The main events of painful drama are unfolded through Michael who even after ten years is not prepared to bury the past and, in fact a chance meeting revives the relationship and the illicit affair is allowed to continue.

The narrator is at pains to unburden his travails and his disillusionment with the city of London:

> London unsettles me—even from such a height. There is no clear countryside to view. But it is not Vienna. It is not Venice. It is not for that matter, home town in the North in clear reach of moors.[11]

Again, in the very next page, we are told of the balance sheet of gain and loss between two of us, resulting in an unequal share of pain: "what I lost there. I have never come near to retrieving."[12]

Suddenly, we are switched back to the events of the past which began on a high pitch of love at first sight but ultimately ending into an unbearable suffering, necessitating the decision of leaving Vienna for Rochdale: "What happened to me many years ago? Love or no love, I could not continue in that city, I stumbled, my mind jammed, I felt the pressure of every breath; I told her I was going and went."[13]

Though the song finally disperses, the agony abides and memories, we are told, are not dead things: "Where are you now, Julia and am I not forgiven?"[14] And his mind, the narrator's mind, wanders to another city, to the memory of another woman, who was as 'as young then.' It is not Virginie but Julia who haunts him like the spirit that exists but eludes. The reflective narrator Michael vividly remembers the circumstances, which resulted in his intimacy with a woman who was, like him, a music student: "If I had not met him, I would not have brought to life the voice in my hands—if I would not have met Julia, I would not have lost Julia."[15]

Besides the memory of Julia and his abortive love, there are other bitter-sweet memories of his struggling parents, the lonely auntie Joan and the gracious lady Mrs. Formby, all of whom ultimately die, leaving him stunned and derelict. However, Julia remains his permanent obsession and even after ten years of gap, when he sees her in a bus, he becomes so desperate in his chase that he loses a precious record in the taxi. He still reads in her eyes the message of love—"not alarm or puzzlement or pity. In that woman's eyes could I read love?"[16]

Apart from the theme of undying love, there is the allied theme of creation of music. 'The theme of point-counterpoint,' 'dying,' 'undying,' a dying fall and a rise and the creation of music in terms of rise and fall of waves and the contribution of the trio—Piers, Helen and Billy, not to mention that of the narrator, is also given prominent emphasis or stress at regular intervals:

> We play in an energized trance and produce those complex vibrations that jog the inner ear and through them the gray mass that produces the complex emotions of joy, love, sorrow, and beauty.[17]

Similarly, much later, when Julia unveils two mysteries about her present life viz. her marriage to James Hansen and the birth of a son called Luke and her loss of hearing, music is once again viewed as a major consolation and solace:

> Music is the heart of my life. For me, of all people, to be betrayed by ears was unbearable.[18]

Again, to Julia, this was a strange transition from the world of sound to the world of deafness—"not soundlessness, really because I hear all sorts of noises, only usually they are the wrong ones."[19]

Finally, Michael learns to live without Julia who realizes that she cannot live a double life any more. Hence after a series of tempestuous adulterous affairs in London and Venice, Michael finally leaves for Rochdale and learns that music alone can sustain him. As Michael eventually realizes, "music, such music is a sufficient gift. Why ask for happiness: Why hope not to grieve? It is enough: it is to be blessed enough, to live from day to day and hear such music—not too much, or the soul could not sustain it—from time to time."[20]

The question now arises if the novel is able to achieve the height of 'equal music,' which the title of the novel points to. Opinion of readers and critics is sharply divided. For Prof. M.K. Naik, the novel fails to achieve integration as a memorable love story. In fact, he advances two reasons. First, the story is 'commonplace' and it has an element of ordinariness. Second, music, far from being an ally of true love, becomes a 'fatal liability.' In fact, he also refers to the third defect that the novel is replete with technical jargons viz. the art of Fugue, Trout, C-minor, and C-major etc, which to an uninitiated reader sound all Greek.[21]

Indeed while there is some point in such criticism, it cannot explain the novel's failure. Basically, the novel's central focus is on the love between two devoted students of music and, in spite of their separation, music sustains them. Moreover, use of quotations, allusions and parallelisms is a common feature of modern literature. Even, Eliot's *The Wasteland* was similarly criticized by the formidable literary critics like F.R. Leavis and Elizabeth Drew on similar grounds and was silenced by Cleanth Brooks and several enlightened Western and Indian critics. Moreover, as a sympathetic reviewer has rightly suggested, there are two kinds of writers—"those driven by the need to say something and those who are motivated by a desire to explore."

Vikram Seth obviously belongs to the latter category and his success or failure is to be judged in that context. Perhaps the present novel does not succeed in making a perfect fusion but no body can deny that, like every great work of art, it makes a fresh raid upon the inarticulate.

NOTES AND REFERENCES

1. Naik, M.K. and Narayan, Shyamala A., *Indian English Literature: 1980-2000: A Critical Survey,* Pentcraft, New Delhi (2001), 40.
2. Paranjape, Makrand R., *Inside and Outside the Whale: Politics and the New Indian English Novel—The New Indian Novel in English: A Study of the 1980s.* Ed. Kirpal, Viney: Allied: Delhi 1990, 220.
3. Sharma, Jyotirmaya. *The Sunday Times of India,* Patna, April 25, 1999, 9.
4. *Ibid.*
5. *Epigraph to An Equal Music*: (John Donne's Sermons): Viking, Penguin India, 1999.
6. Blamires, Harry, *A History of Literary Criticism,* Macmillan (P.B.), 1999: The Classical Age, 16.
7. Rushdie, Salman, An interview with Malcolm Bradbury: *The Sunday Times of India*; Patna April 25, 1999, 9.
8. Goswami, Seema, *The Telegraph* (Graphiti) May 23, 1999, 8.
9. *Ibid.*
10. *An Equal Music*: Viking: Penguin India: 1999, 14.
11. *Ibid.*, 4.
12. *Ibid.*, 5.
13. *Ibid.*, 18.
14. *Ibid.*, 14.
15. *Ibid.*, 86.
16. *Ibid.*, 150.
17. *Ibid.*, 152.
18. *Ibid.*, 181.
19. *Ibid.*, 381.
20. Naik, M.K. and *et. al.*, *Indian English Literature: 1980-2000: A Critical Survey*: Pentacraft, Delhi 2001, 85.
21. Sharma, Joytirmaya, *The Sunday Times of India,* Patna April 25, 1999, 9.

4

A SOCIAL SEMIOTIC STUDY OF SHOBHA DE'S NARRATIVES

PRATIBHA GUPTA

Previous few decades witnessed an upsurge in Indo-Anglican writings. Market is flooded with Indian Literature in English, particularly in the area of narratives. Indian English narratives hold a prominent place in world literature for their intense and esoteric sensibility. Women writers have played prominent role in the area. They get inspiration from their predecessors and emerge as metamorphosed new women, fully aware of their identities, rights, duties, desires, as well as their limitations. They have their own viewpoint about life and do not need a male looking glass to view the matters of their concern. These writers have shed the taboos imposed on them by the chauvinistic male society. They present life in a new color and flavour. Shobha De transforms the identity of Indian women and in her narratives we find a new woman who is actively conscious of her status both at home and outside. Her writings reflect the new women striving hard to attain total freedom.

Feminism in Indian context is a by-product of the western liberation movement in general and feminist thought in particular. The specificity and difference of women's writing is based on a culture, which incorporates ideas about women's body, language, psyche and interprets them in relation to the social context in which they occur. The indigenous contributing factors are equality of sexes, constitutional rights of women, spread of education and the new awareness among women. In Indian feminist narratives there is a considerable variety of women characters' attitude. They are caught in the flux of tradition and modernity saddled with the burden of the past. To slough her passivity and to fulfil her aspirations are the crux of feministic narratives in Indian literature. It precipitates in search for identity and a quest for the definition for the self.

Social semiotics (Hodge and Kress, 1988) incorporates concepts from a wide range of disciplines like, linguistics, sociology, psychology and semiotics. Each of these is concerned with some aspect of the social production of meaning. It includes the study of contexts, purposes, agents and their activities as socially organized structures of meaning, providing strategy that is more intensive, more flexible, more comprehensive, and more committed to the study of social forces constituting the text. De was brought up in a middle class family and spent most of her life in urban society. She experienced fast life style of the materialistic world of metropolis. Her characters belong to the fast moving society of the mad, materialistic world. Their primary concerns are marriage, money and the tangles of human ties. Her women characters are her spokespersons. As study of texts cannot be taken up in isolation, social forces and its agents play decisive role in the process and production of meaning. Crucial aspects of social semiotics, which enrich the bonds of interpretation, are: Social meanings and functions of style, Category of modality and concept of transformation.

The basic concept of Social meanings and function of styles is reflected through structures. Stucturalists took up only structures into consideration and are indifferent to social contexts and processes. But a semiotic structure has a significant relationship between two or more elements, which makes them powerful categories for the study of social meaning. For instance, "Your are behaving like this?" (Second thought, 120). Social meaning of this syntagm is dependent on the set of the paradigmatic choices that it constitutes. The illocutionary force of this structure gets from the paradigmatic choices:

You were from Calcutta/
Families/this environment/
A girl of your sort of background,/etc.

Here functions of style determine the structural genre. In fact style is a distinguishing mark of aesthetics and a decisive factor in the construction of valued literature. Only the choice of structures does not confer a social meaning, but it does only when viewed with reference to social structure. Here the function of style is to represent contempt and not to pose a question. It reflects attitude of men towards womenfolk in Indian society. Even in the so-called modern and progressive society women are still expected to be an ever ready obey-girl. The social forces and agents all exist outside the text that effects each component and signifies something of its semiosic context. It may construct a pseudo-situation as a part of its own mimetic function.

Through these structures De is not putting a carnivalesque query to the patriarchal order. She is working within the terms of language, which has been defined as phallocentric. There is a kind of irony, putting questions to the liberal and advanced patriarchal organisation.

> Of course, she was receiving several calls from other parties, but because you were from Calcutta, she says 'yes.'

Structurally it appears to be acceptance of a proposal, but here by constructing a complex set of author/speaker and reader/hearer, together with the relationship that links them with social meaning it does create a lots of semiosic work. The very first sentence constructs a situation that is true to the Indian situation. It shows that even in the educated and privileged class traditional and orthodox mind is present. It reflects the scornful comment of the speaker. The very word 'Calcutta' signifies the nature of decision. She was chosen not for her superiority over the others but because of her 'roots of tradition.' Structures point out the nature of the atmosphere in the text. Powerful sets of social myths and discriminatory customs have allotted her the role of a passive being in the scheme of things. In mythical terms the dominant feminine prototype is the chaste, patient, self-denying, long-suffering wife.

The sentence is a structural unit with a 'locutionary meaning.' To explore the interpretive power of a text it is necessary to look for social contexts and functions of style.

Category of modalities, *i.e.*, the set of ways that the meaning of texts are keyed into structures of meanings outside them in such a way as to command or disclaim beliefs, determines the functional genre. In terms of semiotics, style is constituted by set of signs and most of these are not verbal. The words 'structure' and 'function' represents two distinct notions. The relationship between structure and function in the study of language and signs are major concerns in humanistic discipline. These two may be easily separated in the abstract, but are not at all easy to study in isolation. One of the most formidable tasks now facing us is that of understanding how structural and functional aspects interrelate in any given instance to produce an interpretation. Since functions cannot be known directly but must be inferred, it would seem to be functions that introduce indeterminacy into systems. Structures encompass both the individual structuring minds with its unique combination of furnishing as well as an internalized public code and the structure of language texts created by individuals working within conventional system. The slanted structures from *Socialite Evenings*:

> We were reduced to being marginal people. Everything that mattered to us was trivialized. The message was "you don't count, except in the context of my priorities." It was taken for granted that our needs were secondary to their. And that in some way we ought to be grateful for having a roof over our head and four square meals a day (69) depict plight of women in a particular society (Indian).

Here Karuna's observations present a stereotype of Indian women. But the illocutionary meaning is that she detests the callous attitude of her husband. Indian males are privileged and have right to shout, abuse, bully, and it is women who tolerate, all these passively. These structures working within the conventional system of Indian society, gets its meaning from the freedom to infer meaning in unlimited number of purposes which are understood by human reasoning and by reference to shared conventions. Shobha's women characters are different. They are not yes persons and bow down in meek subordination. They challenge the male chauvinism. These structures working within the conventional system of

Indian society refers to a different kind of women. The new woman is now aware of her likes and dislikes. Hence expressive categories of modalities in considerations reflects the mind set of these new emerging women. She finds,

> Men like dogs could be conditioned through the reward and punishment (87).

This structure shows that illocutionary force is already embedded in the line itself. It reflects nostalgic hatred towards men. In her very first novel this new woman tries to face the inertia of tradition but the instinctive desire within her makes her uncomfortable and forces her to think over the bondage put upon her. In 'Starry Nights' she portrays Indian women and tries to emphasize that she can have ambitions that is a taboo in Indian society. With regard to the inner craving of women, she crosses the border once thought to be men's territory. The angry young women revolted against the tradition and established their own rules. She has blown away the old beliefs. The idea of marriage and constancy in love has undergone a sea change. Now these women are not prototypes of Sita and Draupadi. They have started venting their thoughts and desires. Women in upper class society in India have grown out of the Victorian taboos. For them physical love outside marriage is not considered out of bonds. De portrays these characters as they are. Hence very often her works are viewed as pornographic and distasteful.

The stucturalist always have done away with author and his intention, but the theory of social semiotic emphasizes the role of underlying systems of conventions. It enables the elements to function as signs. In order to exist, literature, as a social practice, there must be writers, readers and texts. And these three indispensable elements do not normally exit in the same time and place. Therefore the meanings of the semiotic plane (*e.g.*, the author or the reader) are very important aspect of the social meaning of literature. They imply versions of social relations, which serves a crucial ideological function, especially persuasive because they often remain outside that particular text. These can be seen like social facts and meanings that is built up out of syntagmas, messages. These are about elements, processes and relationships on semiotic plane and have both a mimetic content (their version of society) and a semiotic content (sources) within a specific semiotic situation. De's style depicts new women in a mood of revolt. It undermines the old mythologies of gender relationships by questioning and revising them. They are challenging the stereotypes, fairy tales, traditions and histories that are prescribed plots of their lives and estimates their authority and power. She is now like a released, long blocked river sweeping away every thing coming her way. And very often it has devastating effect on the society. But without realizing the psychological current underneath the apparent rudeness her style of writing is blamed for being too open and pornographic. In her last novel that wrath slowly giving way to a meditating and objective observation with a new vision and hope where she says, in *Second Coming*:

So what? I had all the time in the world now (289).

Now she is reconciled to herself. She realizes that she must have her own world and live as per her wish. She should carry out her duties but with dignity and self-respect. The questioning on tradition is the hallmark of her fiction. Cultural maxims, truism and recognizing self-identity are reflected through her fiction. The style is the writer's mode of perception and apprehension of the world about its characters, incidents, nature, environment, experiences and transformation into a verbal construct. Myths are supposed to be socio-cultural coordinates and it gives *locus standi* of the author's perception of reality. She uses Indian myths to create the natural setting.

The literary theories and work of art have always been concerned with complex and problematic relations between texts and their objects. A work of art always tries to transform. In social semiotics these acts of transformation refer to material social events. Transformational analysis is concerned with social agencies and conditions as part of its transformational phenomena. It looks at what and who is doing it and why. In social semiotics, concept of transformation refers to two semiotic acts:

1. act of interpretation that attempts to reconstruct the original act of production,
2. a piece of writing which incorporates the text-as-read into a new text.

As regard to the act of interpretation, in De's fictions the semiotic plane is organized by the set of messages. Due to the different interpretations of readers and sources of these meanings, there is more than a single set of meanings on the semioitic plane. In the bewildering flux of semiotic, syntagms are inscribed into or inerpreted from a text by authors or readers. Her early novels reveal angry young women venting their frustrations and passions. They believe in the tit for tat measures. They make the male folk realize their misconceptions. For them being women does not mean a shy, docile, meek person. She is now bold enough to carry out the acts, which are once thought to be taboo for women. She unveils the real face lurking behind the veil. Her texts offer different interpretations to different readers. On its face her fictions appears to be crude, vulgar but under its surface lies a faithful presentation of the social reality is different from what it appears to be.

The piece of writing that makes a particular text-as-read into a new text creates a New World of its own by elaboration and specifications of the semiotic syntagms and by linking them into new patterns of differences and identity. The thought patterns of Maya in *Second Thoughts* are nearly identical to its source (De's observation on women's plight).

> Why not? Didn't husbands share pleasant nothing with their wives?
>
> Or
>
> Ah! But men—husbands rarely phone their wives just for a chat.... All that lovely talk only takes place during courtship. (208)
>
> Or
>
> Women weren't important to Rajan. They didn't have a validity of their own. He saw them in context to men and family life (225).

But gradually this nagging wife is transformed into a wise and experienced lady with her own guts and she throws away those, which are superfluous and unnecessary. Within the limits of the societal boundaries she creates a world of her owns. She finds the truth that all the men behave in the same way whether he is Nikhil her lover or husband Rajan. Her observations on men's attitude from a wife's point of view, a girl coming from different family, a mimetic construct is created, which has its semiotic effect. It projects De as a social critic challenging the accepted norms of the day. The patterns repeated in her fictions are of tradition and modernism. A recurring motif of romantic idea versus traditional idea is repeated in both its mimetic and semiotic planes. The rating of the texts as best seller indicates the presence of an important semiotic event.

Hence by observing the broad semiotic characters and functions of texts by putting them in the context of general semiotic process De's narratives present powerful social myths. They provide valuable insights into important social meanings and attitudes of the characters working within the social preview. Her characters depict the socio-psychological reason behind the rebellion of her women characters.

WORKS CITED

Ardener, Edwin. Belief and the problem of women in S. Ardener, 'Perceiving Women,' 1975.

De', Shobha. Second Thoughts. Penguin Books, 1996.

——. Socialite Evenings, 1989.

——. Starry Nights, 1991.

Frye, Northrop. Analogy of criticism: Four essays Princeton, N.J. Garvin, Paul, trans. & ed., A Prague school Reader on Esthetics, Literary structure & style, Washington DC, 1964.

Hodge R. and Kress G. Social semiotic, Oxford, Polity Press, 1988.

Searle, J.R. 'A classification of illocutionary acts' Language in society, 1976.

Swain. S.P., Todorov, Tzvtan. 'The Origin of Genres,' NLH 8, 1976.

5

AN ANALYSIS OF ANITA DESAI'S MAYA AS 'A PURE WOMAN'

ANITA PARIHAR

Toto's death in *Cry, The Peacock*, casts a shadow of death over the whole novel. Maya's scream at Toto's death merges with the shrill cry of the peacocks and her early sense of horror turns into a nightmare as the novel progresses. The fear that grips her at the moment of Toto's death, gives shape to a shadowy, hazy vision—a vision which she is not able to etch clearly and identify but which fills her with a sense of "strange horror" (Desai: 1980: 8) not connected with the corpse of her pet dog, as she thought at first, but with an agonizingly disturbing experience at some point of time in her life: "known, and forgotten...at one time, feared, and now rediscovered" (27). This vision, which goes out of focus momentarily, is back at night, haunting her—a shadowy presence, very real, a "truly physical shadow" which is inexplicable and an "undefinable unease" (12) grips her and this "strange unease" (27) grows, reaching a distressing point causing her to leap in terror:

> ...and I leapt from my chair in terror, overcome by a sensation of snakes coiling and uncoiling their moist lengths about me, of evil descending from an overhanging branch, of an insane death, unprepared for, heralded by deafening drum-beats... (13).

The dark, intensely black night, the star spangled sky, with "spaces of darkness" (22) only intensify her sense of loneliness and death. The constellation-hieroglyphs do not provide her an answer to the strange restlessness that she feels. The presence of the dark shadow in the meantime is more deeply felt:

> ...a distant apprehension of a presence. Like an undercurrent beneath the throbbing of drums, a foreign odour amidst the scent of lemon blossoms... (27).

The stars fail to give her an answer. The moon however provides her with the answer. The past opens up and explains the shadowy presence:

> In the end, it was not the stars that told me, but the moon, when it rose out of the churn of my frenzy, vast and ghost-white,...it was not the gentle moon of love ballads and fairy revels...but a demoniac creature, the fierce dancer that had all day been trying to leap the threshold of my mind and home, accompanied by a deafening roar of silent drums. It was the mad demon of Kathakali ballads, masked, with heavy skirts swirling, feet stamping, eyes shooting beams of fire. It was a phantom gone berserk... (27-28).

The shadow—"black and evil" is not the demon in a Kathakali dance, nor is it the phantom on the moon but identifiable through these figures. He is the albino priest—'Fate' whom she had encountered as a child. She remembers his "pale, opaque" (28) eyes and his oily finger pointing at the unseen mark on her forehead—a mark which signified 'Death'—Death 'Four years after...marriage' he had predicted—by 'unnatural causes' to 'one of you,' (30) he had concluded. The paralysing terror of childhood is relived again. As a child, she saw the priest as a "fearsome magician" (32) but now he is sheer 'Evil' to her—The childhood terror turns into a nightmare for she has been married to Gautama for four years.

It is spring—Maya's inner world suddenly transforms—as evident in her response to the sound and colour of the world around her. The "scarlet blooms" of cotton are "blood-blobs" (34) to her; the twittering of baby pigeons exasperates her and the 'Coo' of the doves are "frantic warnings" (35) to her. The brain-fever bird's "mournful cry" (34) upsets her. The relentless disquiet and the feverish restlessness that she feels is reflected in an atmosphere also "charged with restlessness" (35).

She recalls "another spring"—an "idyllic one" which stands in contrast to the present one. She recalls the "bougainvillea arbour" in her father's house, loaded with blossoms. It not only provided shade, but was a magic spot, which with the play of light changed from "lilac to mauve to purple, from peach to orange to crimson" (36)—so different from the "thorny paper flowered bougainvillea creepers" (35) in her husband's garden—whose dry rattle unnerved her. Spring in Lucknow brought with it bright, orange flecked butterflies and "ecstatic insects" (36) and "brilliant grasshopper[s]" and "velvet bugs"—sending a thrill through her, a delight which made her "drowsy" (37) while the spring at Lucknow is symbolic of her delirious joy and happiness the present spring is symbolic of her inner tremulous disquiet.

But Maya is not in her father's house. She is surrounded by Gautama's family. They are engrossed in political discussion, which does not interest her in the least. She is a woman who is close to nature, instinctual, sensitive. She wishes to draw the family into her world but there was not one amongst them to whom she could turn and cry out, 'Look, Look—there is a moon in the sky!' (51). She even yearns for human contact, even if it were to kiss "each separate calloused knuckle" of Gautama's mother, or keep holding the baby—"rejoicing in its weight." The unfulfilled desire remains a futile longing:

> Now, when I surged, open armed, towards them, all receded to some distant background...I ardently and futilely longed... (52).

A Lawrentian character, anti-intellectual, sensitive, and her body a "flame" (Daleski: 1965: 62).

> But there was a moon. A great moon of hot, beaten copper, of molten brass, livid and throbbing like a bloody human organ, a great, full-bosomed woman who had mounted the skies in passion, driven the silly stars away from her, while she pulsed and throbbed, pulsed and glowed across the breathless sky (51).

Maya, with the "translucent skin" and the "blue flashing veins" beneath the opal ring, waiting for Gautama, who gave no thought to her "soft willing body" (9) is like the moon-lonely and alienated. He is not "conscious of the swell of [her] hip" (42).

He has a "pontifical air" (146) about him—he is like a judge or like a "mediator beneath the *bo* tree" (113) and Maya, is hungry for a touch of his finger—for one such touch, a rare moment was to her the "velvet well of the primordium, of original instinct, of first formed love" (11). There are moments when she is desirous but afraid to make a "bold, physical move." There are moments when she wants to "draw him into [her] own orbit of thought and feeling" (41). What is her orbit? It is not simply a desire for physical contact—it encompasses the entire world of nature. She lives in the open air and takes as much delight in the "curved arc of a birds wing" as in the "steam rising from a pot of tea" (91). The "untrained voice" heard on a moonlit night fills her with immense joy and the "odour of a ripe pineapple" (92) sends a thrill through her while the sight of the warm "sun unfurl" (105) drowns her in sheer ecstasy. She wishes to share this with Gautama—"contact that goes deeper than flesh" (104). But Gautama is different. He never responds to the beauty of nature—he cannot distinguish between the fragrance emitted by a bed of Petunias and the lemon blossoms. His world is the world of books, legal cases, politics, philosophy and occasionally poetry. She is aware of the difference in their world:

> ...it seemed to me that I was climbing a mountain from the top of which could be seen the entire world, unfolded like a map, with sun—silkened trees and milk—mild rivers and jewelled townships amidst fields of grain and valleys and tracts, all fruitful, all florescent. While he, because he did not care for walks, or views, remained behind in the dusty, enclosed cup of the small plain down below (91).

But now, with the death of Toto, and the figure of the albino priest haunting her, she needs him—his companionship and understanding. She has a strong desire to confess her "terror of loneliness" but then concluded that it would be "Useless, Hopeless" (27). Withdrawn, isolated, she begins to live with the "shadow of the dancer" (52) which brings a drastic transformation in her life. Living in perpetual fear, which intensifies at the party, when she overhears the word 'Fate'—a word she had not heard for years—is now "burningly mnemonic" (76) and the Sikh gentleman who had uttered the word merges into the figure of the albino priest:

> He laughed jovially. So jovially that an alliance with the albino of the black and oil slick temple gate was discounted immediately (77-78).

She shrinks in fear when he "reaches out" his "square, hairy" hand to read her destiny for he is an ally of that "magician of the underworld, the albino, his shadow." When he rivets his attention on her, again and again, her distress mounts and the "distraught tenseness" (79) is clearly visible on her face. Ultimately she is seized by intense fear for she detects in him the same menacing 'evil' as in the priest:

> ...this time I detected in his leer something of the lascivious evil in the smiles and gestures of the albino astrologer, and I perspired freely in panic (80).

'Fate'—the "one word set playing again the mysterious leitmotiv" filling her with "insane fear" (80). The words "Fatality-fate, Fate-fatality" (94) haunt her constantly, ceaselessly and her world is "tainted with fatality" (4) and there is no escape from the memory of the albino-priest:

> I summoned up again the vision of the tenebrific albino who had cast his shadow like a net across me as I had fled down the corridor of years, from the embrace of protection to the embrace of love, yet catching me as surely as a giant fisherman striding through the shadows of moonlit seas, throws his fine net with one brief, express motion and knows, as it settles with a falling whisper upon the still water, that he will find in it a catch: I had not escaped (94-95).

Release from this image seems impossible to her as words fall from his "oil-slick, sibilant tongue" whispering to her, telling her about the cry, of the peacocks—their "blood-chilling" shrieks which "like Shiva's,...dance of joy is the dance of death" (95) and now Maya's own dance of life, is to her, the dance of death—she identifies herself with the peacocks:

> In the shadows I saw peacocks dancing, the thousand eyes upon their shimmering feathers gazing steadfastly, unwinkingly upon the final truth—Death. I heard their cry and echoed it. I felt their thirst as they gazed at the

> rain—clouds, their passion as they hunted for their mates. With them, I trembled and panted and paced the burning rocks. Agony, agony, the mortal agony of their cry for lover and for death.

Maya "wept for them, and wept for [herself]," knowing their words to be [hers] and so the cry, of the peacocks from the "rocky waste land" of old Delhi, set her "crying the peacock's cry" (97). Her world is transformed. Maya, turns inwards—and the terrifying dark inner world in which she is imprisoned is the reverse of the world of colour and sound which she so loved. At this juncture she feels that Gautama's world has changed. Seeing him with friends in the garden she thinks:

> Already we belonged to separated worlds, and his seemed the earth that I loved so, scented with jasmine, coloured with liquor, resounding with poetry and warmed by amiability. It was mine that was hell. Torture guilt, dread, imprisonment—these were the four walls of my private hell, one that no one could survive in long. Death was certain (102).

She, however, has a strong desire to live:

> Father! Brother! Husband! Who is my saviour? I am in need of one. I am dying, and I am in love with living, I am in love and I am dying (98).

The "ecstasy of being alive"— (103) to fulfill her deep longing for Gautama: 'to touch him, feel his flesh and hair, hold and then tighten [her] hold on him.' She also loves the 'pulsating world around him' (102). But Maya's inner world is turning into a chaotic one in which the "thundering drums" (123) turn deafening. She feels suffocated and the sense of uncertainty haunts her: 'But to perish? Who? Tell me who?' (125). Images of death in the shape of a "viper's fang;" "flap jawed ape;" and lizards "stalking...silently" their "audible hiss" a "death's rattle" (127) haunt her. The lizard image is the strongest and persists for a longer time, perhaps because she recalls the albino-priest "flicking [his] garment...flicking it as a lizard flicks its tongue at a petrified victim" (32). The malevolent image haunts her, even when she momentarily comes out of the inner world:

> 'what are these lizards called, Gautama—the big ones that walk on their toes? Like alligators, almost.'
> 'Iguanas?'
> 'Iguanas?' My blood ran cold, and I heard the slither of its dragging tail even now, in white daylight. 'Get off I tell you, get off! Go!' (128).

She sits as "in a tomb" (129) waiting for death. She waits while the drumbeats grow in "strength and volume" (145)—drumbeats which "never ceased" (151). Gautama's concern about her horoscope triggers off more relentlessly the "sound of drums, drums beating" (150-151). She feels she is turning insane. But cutting across this inner world—a world of hallucinations we see in her a growing sense of caution. The mystery surrounding her horoscope is to be kept a secret, never to be told as new dangers would arise:

> Ah, if Gautama found out, would he, might he not put me in peril of my life? Did he not love life too, its problems.... The mystery, the mystery. Soft, soft, with care now Maya, with care (151).

She is afraid to be alone with Gautama who is her "unknowing, unsuspecting and steel hard adversary in this oneiric battle." There is now no respite for her. She is alone-afraid of the silent dark room and the "ghost-white moon" (163) which watched her constantly. She begins to feel the need once again to be close to Gautama—even complains to him that he does not console her, speak to her or even walk with her in the evenings, which was a daily ritual. She cannot overcome her loneliness. Her sleepless nights are filled with "frenzied cries of the peacocks" and the night sky turns into a "flurry of peacocks' tails, each star a staring eye"—Gautama hears nothing. She draws her conclusion:

> The man had no contact with the world, or with me. What would it matter to him if he died and lost even the possibility of contact? What would it matter to him? It was I, I who screamed in mute horror (175).

It is not only Gautama who cannot comfort or, understand her. Her father's "gentle words" that had once cheered her, meant nothing to her now. Arjuna's name "sounded unfamiliar" (176). The only words which she recalls are the ones uttered by the albino—'It cannot be altered, you must accept'—words, which pursue her to the point where she is "torn between two worlds—the receding one of grace, the approaching one of madness" (177).

Finally, she cries out, "All order, is gone out of my life, all formality." The fear of death is followed by the fear of the nature of death "will it be fire? Will it be flood?" or, will the "lizards rise out of the desert to come upon us" (179). She is so disturbed that she cannot discriminate the voices of the birds—"which is the hoopoe's, which the doves?" and this is strange for one who was so close to nature, who could distinguish one odour from another, one song of the bird from that of another. She is tired, restless and then panic grips her as she looks at the "death-like tiles of the terrace below" (180). Why does she panic? The thought of 'murder' crosses her mind. Early in the novel this word is used by Maya and it points towards her future thought and act. She tells Gautama:

> And why must it always be money? It's always money, or property—never a case of passion and revenge! Murder and exciting things like that (20).

The word 'murder' follows her as "well-aimed arrow" and at times she even "paused to feel the arrow of that word, murder" (166).

Maya has finalized her plan to murder Gautama. Calm descends on her. This is reflected through the hushed silence that descends all round her before the storm:

> Nothing could move. No leaf could stir, no blade of grass. The homely insects, the birds, bees, worms of the garden, where were they all? (183).

The "lizards were still" the ants "silent" (182) and "each ear-snail's, lion's, shark's" was "listening for that final, awful crash." (181) The scene outside Maya's window changes in hue from "darkening-harsh yellow...to bitter ochre" (183) and from "olive haze to...purulent purple." "Hot, harsh colours, like a vulture's impatient screams" (184)—colours which she identifies with her own murderous thought and her guilt:

> A force was altering it into some thing fierce, strange, lurid, a macabre cartoon with which to frighten

> those innocent and more so, infinitely more so, those guilty (184).

Maya, however, is waiting for the "end, the ultimate, the final vision of the final fate" and that "had to appear now" (184) and in a "camera of insanity" she sees the "future insanity":

> ...beyond the window...guilt, sin, crime, punishment all stood stock still, struck into threatening immobility by a ruthless force of fate (185).

The storm brings with it a sense of immense joy. The "infidel storm" to her signifies "release and liberty." She runs from "room to room, laughing as maniacs laugh." She is no longer afraid:

> Frightened? No! I ran from the thought laughing Oh no, what need for fright? It is relief, I called back to the gods who mocked in the dark wings, it is only relief at having survived, at having regained the will and the decision to survive. It is only relief. I promise you, you shall see—I swear survive... (190).

She is to live and it is Gautama who is to die. She even justifies her decision when she mentions the storm and Gautama snaps back '...What storm?' (194):

> All that I felt now at his surprise was resignation and even relief. It had only underlined unawareness, a half-deadness to the living world, which helped and strengthened me by justifying my decision (195).

She walks beside him in the lawn and thinks of him as an "unreal ghost" and as a "body without a heart, a heart without a body" (196). She knows he lives "so narrowly, so shallowly" (196-197) and is also aware of the fact that he is a "harmless, guiltless" person. It seems that she is sympathetic towards him and is willing to give him a chance to live by changing her decision. She recalls his indifferent attitude towards Toto's death and decides to talk about his death once more: 'It seems such a long time since Toto died. I don't know why—whenever I see these lime tress—I miss him, so much?' (197). She waits eagerly for his response. But Gautama has already forgotten Toto: 'Toto? Who was that?' he asks. She begs him to answer once more, as if giving him one last chance to live—but he fails to do so and so she passes her verdict: "The words were as grim as any death sentence, absolute and unredeemable." If he had given a sympathetic response "all might have been quite different" (198), she admits.

To justify her murderous thought Maya analyses at length her life with Gautama and concludes:

> ...but it was Gautama who found many more things to teach that heart, new, strange and painful things. He taught it pain, for there were countless nights when I had been tortured by a humiliating sense of neglect, of loneliness, of desperation that would not have existed had I not loved him so, had he not meant so much (201).

Her painful existence is subjected to further analysis:

> There never lived a bird that did not know a storm, a stone, a wound. And I, an adult, thinking woman, had no more right to happiness than I had been taught by Gautama, to regard as a privilege (201-202).

Her plan is already chalked out and she leads Gautama to the deathtrap. She changes the venue of their daily routine evening walk:

> 'No!' I cried, springing into action, springing to keep him from turning into the garden. 'Gautama, let us go up the roof instead shall we?' (203).

She discloses her mind by giving oblique hints. For instance, she confides "Having achieved this...my excitement...now subsided..." (203). While climbing up the steps, Gautama's comment with reference to the cat having a 'guilty conscience...' to Maya is a "pinpointed weapon" (204) which does not scathe her. She has overcome all fear. She is calm and collected. They walk on the roof, from one end to the other and she is consciously waiting for an opportunity to push Gautama over the edge and she waits for the opportune moment "now and then [they] passed at the edge of the roof, but not too close" (205). They walk the stretch of the roof again and again. She is exhausted, but she is determined to act: "yet I could not pause, could not dream of pausing now" (207). Gautama, innocently talks about his legal case and Krishnan, and all the while Maya feels sorry for him, but yet, her decision does not change: "Gautama...had never lived, and never would" (208) she decides. She has chalked out her plan she just waits for the right moment, the right opportunity.

A deliberate and conscious manipulation on the part of Anita Desai, makes things fall into place. It is a strange coincidence that Maya should pause at the edge of the parapet and make Gautama pause as well at the right spot. The moon rises for the third and final time. The moon, not demonic and pulsating and throbbing, but a moon symbolic at once of mother-love and purity:

> ...it appeared a great multifoliate rose, waxen white, virginal, chaste and absolute white, casting a light that was holy in its purity, a soft suffusing glow of its chastity, casting its reflection upon the night with a vast, tender mother love (208).

The moon, as a chaste woman, is identifiable with Diana, the moon-goddess of chastity who is also identified with Artemis. The mythical basis is evident here. The moon reflects, as intended by Anita Desai, the soul of Maya. This symbolic reference to Maya as a pure woman, as a chaste woman, full of motherly love comes just before the murder. Gautama, comes between the "worshipped moon" and Maya-transgressing its "sorrowing chastity" (208). He is pushed down to his death by Maya.

Maya is childless. However, the moon, in its final symbolic role appears as a 'mother figure'—of course, reflecting Maya's tender mother-love for Gautama. She admits earlier:

> I melted with tenderness, my arms curled into an instinctive cradle, a possessive embrace, as I went, over thoughts of him (92-93).

Luxuriating in this tender mother feeling she elaborates:

> If mothers enjoy watching the clumsy drooling of their babes while they eat, or their faltering attempts at walking, then I enjoyed, similarly, his helplessness...his speechless need of me... (93).

'Both in myth and in life the roles of mother and wife overlap' (Ferguson: 1973:7) and Maya is projected in this dual role. It may be mentioned that as a wife she harbours a mother's tender love towards Gautama, which of course, is never overtly expressed, just as a wife she never expresses her love for him.

As a mother-figure we see her in the context of Myths. For "Myths about woman's dual nature are attempts to explain primordial reactions to her double role" (Ferguson: 1973: 7) which gives the woman a "negative and a positive" (6) side. Here, when we see the negative aspect of Maya, we see her only as a hardened murderer. The question arises, can Maya be identified as a chaste woman, a pure woman, as the moon symbolizes. This question brings to mind Hardy's Tess as 'A pure woman'—the subtitle so befitting in the interpretation of Maya's character as well. Tess in Hardy's *Tess of the D'urbervilles*, kills Alec in a sudden fit of rage and passion. The pain and agony in her voice testifying her sudden emotionally charged act:

> And he is dying—he looks as if he is dying!...And my sin will kill him and not kill me!...Oh, you have torn my life all to pieces—made me be what I prayed you in pity not to make me be again!...My own true husband will never, never—Oh, God—I can't bear this! I cannot!" (Hardy: 1993: 402).

Maya, however, does not kill on impulse. She has planned out the brutal murder of her husband. And, like the Duke, in Browning's "My last Duchess" she is not emotionally disturbed by her act. She recounts to Gautama's mother and sister Nila, the "story of mad horror, all in the same cool, honeyed tones" (213) while serving them tea (which obviously lies cold in front of them) and continues talking:

> ...And when I went down the stairs to the terrace, he was lying there—don't you like your tea? Shall I bring you lemonades instead? It is a hot day? (214).

She also discloses what led her to commit the crime:

> It had to be one of us, you see, and it was so clear that it was I who was meant to live. You see, to Gautama it didn't really matter. He didn't care, and I did (215-216).

Her disclosure is followed by "smiles" and "caresses" (216). The murderous act was obviously committed in a trance like state, a state between sanity and insanity. She seems to be recounting every thing in a trance like state. Once she is out of this state, her in law's hear a "different voice calling, shrilly and desperately, from some unimaginable realm of horror, calling out in great dread." She is back in the world of reality—her smiles stop—the chilling scream is proof of her 'total recall.' The albino-priest's prediction turns out to be partially true. The only thing that is wholly true is that the priest was an evil force which destroyed not one, but two lives. Maya, is pure and chaste to the extent that she plans and executes the murder, in a trance-like state and admits to her crime in that state. The shadow of the albino-priest hangs over her death as well, but the powerful driving force at the end is the realization of the act—the realization of 'guilt, sin, crime, punishment'—which strike her with full force. There is no doubt that Anita Desai, wishes us to see Maya as 'a pure woman' for even when she jumps to her death she is drawn as a 'white figure' (218) and recalls the 'white figure' of Tess at the May dance, though the situations are different in both the novels. The colour white in Hardy's *Tess of the D'urbervilles* stands for purity and so does it, in Anita Desai's novel. Maya and Tess murder—but both are projected as innocent and pure women. There is no doubt that their acts are the result of deep seated anguish as they are both in the grip of two 'Evil' forces—The albino priest and Alec D'urberville—both of whom are responsible for the turbulence in their lives. Their act at one level, may be interpreted as an act of self-liberation—so beautifully brought out by Anita Desai through the "bronze Shiva":

> And yet there was nothing frozen or immobile in this pose of eternal creative movement. The powerful, slightly bent leg and the firm rooting of the graceful foot upon the squirming body of evil, and the raised leg with its arched food, raised into a symbol of liberation... (203).

However, the act of self-liberation in both cases turned out poignantly to be 'liberation' in reality rather than only in a symbolic sense-making them stand out more forcefully as pure women.

WORKS CITED

Desai, Anita, *Cry, The Peacock*. New Delhi: Orient Paperbacks, 1980.

Daleski, H.M., *The Forked Flame: A Study of D.H. Lawrence*. London: Faber and Faber Ltd., 1965.

Ferguson, Anne. *Images of Women in Literature.* Boston: Houghton, 1973.

Hardy, Thomas. *Tess of the D'urbervilles: A Pure Woman.* New Delhi: UBSPD, 1993.

6

A BEND IN THE GANGES AND GANDHI'S PHILOSOPHY OF NON-VIOLENCE

AMBUJ KUMAR SHARMA

Malgonkar ranks amongst the most distinguished Indian English novelists. His novels, short stories and works of non-fiction have been appreciated by his readers and critics all over the world. His *A Bend in the Ganges* won laurels for him and was lauded by E.M. Forster as: 'fine novel written in English by an Indian. Powerful character drawing. Action that ranges from domestic to national bloodshed' (back cover page). The novel moves around Gandhiji's ideology of non-violence and passive resistance.

In *A Bend in the Ganges,* Malgonkar appears to have believed non-violence as the weapon of the weak and meek and violence as an inevitable occurrence in the struggle of life. Shafi Usman alias Singh comments in the novel: "Non-violence is the philosophy of sheep, a creed for cowards. It is the greatest danger to the country" (23). Though the novel begins with the burning of British garments all over the country on the call of Mahatma Gandhi, the 'apostle of truth and non-violence', Yet, later on, it appears to be an incontrovertible evidence of the failure of Gandhiji's ideals of non-violence. The central character Gian Talwar, a true Gandhian and a staunch believer of his ideals of non-violence and truth in the opening pages of the novel, soon becomes an 'angry young man' a killer. A man who worshipped Gandhiji like a God (22) and for whom he was the only man who could win freedom for his country, soon discarded his principles of non-violence.

In the second chapter of *A Bend in the Ganges,* "The Green Flash at Sunset," Gian retorts as a reaction to Singh's taunts: "Ahimsa is the noblest creed.... There can be nothing more sacred. No man has the right to raise his hands against another, whatever the provocation I shall never do it. It takes greater courage; non-violence is not for the weak" (24).

But, ironically, he kills Vishnu Dutt, the only heir of the 'Big House,' with the same axe with which Vishnu Dutt killed his brother Hari, at the end of the seventh chapter, "Bullocks and Bangles" of the novel.

Malgonkar has based this novel on Ghandhiji's doubts about the success and longevity of the ideology of non-violence which he has quoted as an epigraph to the novel:

> This non-violence, therefore, seems to be due mainly to our helplessness. It almost appears as if we are nursing in our bosoms the desire to take revenge the first time we get the opportunity. Can true, voluntary non-violence come out of this seeming forced non-violence of the weak? It is not a futile experiment I am conducting? What if when the fury bursts, not a man, woman, or a child is safe and every man's hand is raised against the neighbour?

The novelist has proved Gandhiji's doubts about the practicability of non-violence to be true in the novel by giving a prefatory note:

> Only the violence in the story happens to be true; it came in the wake of freedom, to become a part of India's history. What was achieved through non-violence, brought with it one of the bloodiest upheavals of history: twelve million people had to flee, leaving their houses; nearly half a million were killed; over a hundred thousand women, young and old, were abducted, raped, mutilated (Author's Note).

Even the Mahatma was not certain about the fate of non-violence. At occasions he himself realized the futility of his experiment with non-violence when he himself witnessed the scenes of violence and fury in his own country. He had a doubt about an hypothetical ideology in an age when the people were on the war path 'experiencing the terrific conclusions of unimaginable fratricidal strife' (Iyengar 432).

Malgonkar has succinctly referred to the root cause of the country's slavery—racial differences amongst the Hindus, Muslims and Sikhs:

> Religious differences among the races of India were root cause of the country's slavery, and the British had learnt to take the fullest advantage of these differences, playing the Hindus against the Muslims and Sikhs against both (78).

The British took the maximum advantage of the racial differences and added fuel to fire by poisoning them against each other. The 'fervent patriots' whose secret mode of greeting was 'Jai-Ram' answered by 'Jai-Rahim' (76-77) and who not only shared their foods but also shared their emotions, in no time, became eternal enemies. Shafi Usman and Hafiz, who jointly fought with Debi Dayal and Basu against the atrocious rule of the British, by the indulgence of some fanatic Muslims and Hindus became enemies for ever. Referring to Jinah's warnings, Hafiz says to Shafi:

> 'I am not a Leaguer only because the League does not believe in our methods'. But there is no denying that Jinah is a great man. He has pointed out the way. We must now turn our back on the Hindus, otherwise we shall become their slaves! His fists were clenched; his nose quivered with passion; drops of spittle flow out of his mouth (94).

The novelist appears to be ironical in his prefatory note when he writes 'what was achieved through non-violence, brought with it one of the bloodiest upheavals of history.' All the characters described as freedom fighters in the novel are basically violent, despising Gandhiji's philosophy of non-violence. Characters like Debidayal, Basu, Hafiz and Shafi consider the followers of non-violence as the 'enemies of the nation' and non-violence as detrimental to the freedom struggle:

> They had nothing but contempt for the non-violent agitation of Mr. Gandhi and his followers; the white men, they were convinced, would never respect such object passivity. To them, the apostles of non-violence were the

> enemies of the nation, bent on emasculating the population (77).

At several places in *A Bend in the Ganges* the violent freedom fighters criticize Gandhiji and his ideology of non-violence. Debidayal believes that the freedom could only be achieved and the British could only be driven out through violence and discards Gandhiji and Nehruji and their passive supporters for their pacifism:

> If only the Gandhis and the Nehrus would discard their pacifism now and channel their energies towards driving out the British with violence, using the terrorists' methods, they could make short wash work of the Raaj.
>
> But they would never do it. They were even more bent on emasculating the nation than the British were (167).

Debidayal believes that the British could only be thrown out by coercion. He laughs at Gandhiji's call of 'Quit India' and comments disguised as Kaluram:

> 'Quit India!' It had almost made him laugh. The British had left Malaya and Burma, but certainly not in response to such slogans. Those who had called on them to quit were not languishing in prison. The British would never quit a country just because a lot of men dressed in dhotis and white caps implored them to do so. The appeal could be regarded as either pathetic or ludicrous, according to whether you were Indian or British. The British would give in only to force. If only the terrorist movement had gone on and had flared up as widely throughout the country as Gandhi's non-violent agitation seemed to have done. This would have been the time for the final assault on the British (277-78).

Basu, another active member of the terrorist group, also condemns Gandhiji's ideology of non-violence like the other members of their group and advocates the use of violence against violence. He comments scornfully about non-violence and calls it 'a dream of philosophers.' Referring to Gandhiji's doubts and fears about non-violence, he says: 'Unless we are prepared to meet violence with violence, we will perish.' If our answer to Muslim fury is to be non-violence, then we shall be slave race again—within weeks of the British leaving us (299). Shafi Usman refutes the principles of Gandhiji at several places in the novel. At one place in the eighth chapter, "Angry Young Man," he goes to the extent of saying that non-violence is an insult to the land which sometimes belonged to great Shivaji, Akbar and Ranjeet. Referring to Jalianwala Bagh massacre, he comments:

> Every one had to go on fours; Shafi had told them. 'Like dogs!—all of us, men, women, children—no one was exempt. That is the sort of insult we have to avenge. And than we talk of non-violence! The creed of non-violence is a voked insult to the land of Shivaji and Akbar and Ranjeet (80).

The words spoken by Usman alias Singh came to be true who announced like a prophet, "A million shall die—a million!" (23), when partition took the shape of religious civil war which engulfed the whole country in an unparalleled holocaust and carnage in the annals of Indian history as Malgonkar describes it with an explicit realism:

> Every citizen was caught up in the holocaust. No one could remain aloof; no one could be trusted to be impartial. When men and women of your religion were being subjected to atrocities, and you could not be expected to remain friendly with adherents of the religion of the oppressors. The administration, the police, even the armed forces, were caught up in the blaze of hatred. Willy-nilly, everyone had come to be a participant in what was, in effect, a civil war. Tens of millions of people had to flee, leaving every thing behind; Muslims from India, Hindus and Sikhs from the land that was soon to become Pakistan: two great rivers of humanity flowing in opposite directions along the pitifully inadequate roads and railways, jamming, clashing, colliding head-on, leaving dead and dying littering the landscape.
>
> As a background to this great, two-way migration, religious civil war was being waged all over the country; a war fought in every village and town and city where two communities came upon each other. The most barbaric cruelties of primitive man prevailed over all other human attributes. The administration had collapsed, the railways

> had stopped functioning because the officials and technicians had themselves joined the mass migrations. Mobs ruled the streets, burning, looting, killing, dishonouring women and mutilating children... (341-42).

The land of five rivers became the land of carrions, the vultures, jackals and crows gnawing and tearing the human flesh (70). The dead bodies were mutilated and disfigured by the vultures, jackals and crows and it became difficult to identify them even in broad-day-light. There was a 'sense of devastation on both sides as though denuded by swarms of locusts or by invading armies' (370) In the thirtieth chapter, "Founder Members," Basu also foresees the inevitability of a racial civil war between Hindus and Muslims: "The moment the British quit, there will be civil war in the country, a great slaughter. Every city, every village, every bustee where the two communities live side by side, will be the scene of war" (299-300).

Being an army officer, Malgonkar, perhaps, could not accentuate Gandhiji's philosophy of non-violence as his ears were attuned to the sounds of gunfires. Therefore, he naturally affirmed to vanquish violence by the weapon of violence. In *A Bend in the Ganges,* Malgonkar, through his violent characters like Shafi, Debidayal and Basu, has tried to enunciate his inclination towards violence. Through these characters, he has tried to establish his point of view that non-violence is a shield of cowards. Gian Talwar, a central character, a non-violent weak and sheepish boy could not muster up his courage to face Vishnu Dutt who was going to attack his brother, Hari:

> But he did not want to go on. He wished to hang back, to run away, to leave this evil place and never to see it again. This was not his fight; it was Hari's, their father's grand father Dada's. His was the path of non-violence— the non-violence of the strong, he reminded himself, arising from courage, not cowardice (52-53).

In the last line of the above quotation, Gian realizes that his non-violence was not the non-violence of the cowards. But when Vishnu Dutt plunged his axe into Hari's head, "Gian felt faint with weakness, the fear inside him bloated like a balloon, choking him, bringing out his breath in short gasps, blinding his eyes. His knees tumbled" (53-54). He soon realized that his non-violence was the non-violence of a coward. He felt guilty and faint-hearted:

> Gian brooded, sick with guilt. 'Coward!...coward!' he kept accusing himself, fanning the flame. Was that why he had embraced the philosophy of non-violence without question—from physical cowardice, not from courage? Was his non-violence merely that of the rabbit refusing to confront the hound? (54).

Most of the Malgonkar's characters in the novel don't believe in non-violence. Majority of the characters in *A Bend in the Ganges* like Debidayal, Shafi Usman, Basu, Hafiz, Ramoshi etc., despise non-violence. It was only Gian who was the true worshipper of Gandhiji and believed that the freedom of India could only be achieved through the path of non-violence and passive resistance. Gian who 'came from an orthodox Hindu background; in his world the sacred thread was still sacred (20), forced by circumstances, he too became a violent, a killer in the beginning of the story. The transformation of Gian from a true-non-violent to a violent supports the failure and hollowness of non-violence preached by Gandhiji. A man of non-violence soon became violent when he got 'the opportunity' and realized that he was a coward. He also realized that non-violence was a weapon specially forged by Gandhiji to fight against the British (66) and declared that 'Hari would not have died if I had what I should' (67).

A Bend in the Ganges explicates the double conflict—conflict between Indian nationalism and British colonialism and conflict between Hindus and Muslims (Iyengar 431). The novel "is to be viewed as the advance micro-tragedy foreshadowing the macro-tragedy on a national scale..." (Iyengar 433). The family feud between the Big House and the Little House is followed by a freedom struggle and a civil war between the Hindus and the Muslims.

In the beginning, Gian Talwar represents Gandhiji's ideology of non-violence. He realizes that 'non-violence is the non-violence of brave, arising not from cowardice but from courage, demanding greater sacrifices than ordinary fighting man are called upon to make (12). But when his brother, Hari, is killed by his cousin Vishnudutt, he feels guilty and brands himself a 'coward.' To satisfy his feelings of 'guilt' and 'cowardice,' he kills Vishnudutt with the 'same axe' and acts against his own words—'whatever the provocation, I shall never do it' (24). Here Gian represents the majority of people who do not stick to their vows and breach them when the occasion demands. Though he is a central character in the novel, but he is not able to control his feelings and desires and acts as an ordinary man. To gratify his feelings he kills Vishnudutt. To fulfil his selfish motto, he cuts the dead man's (Ramoshi's) throat for his gold:

> For a moment, he felt sorry for then, these people who were being so good to him, permitting him such an intimate glimpse of their lives; he was planning to feed upon their distress. But he shook the thought away. This was no time to be squeamish. He had not shrunk from cutting a dead man" throat for his gold. Now it was the relatively simpler matter for playing on the anxiety of man and his wife (242).

He plays with Sundari, the wife of Gopal and betrays his old friend, Debidayal by taking his rupees sent by Sundari and by spying on his movements in the jail. The other important character, Debidayal, in a way is better than Gian who remains what he is. But, we can also put some big question marks on him, *i.e.* his sleeping with his own sister, Sundary, and his taking away of Mumtaz, the beloved of Shafi Usman to avenge upon him.

Before the conversion of Gian from non-violent to violent, there is a conflict in the novel between non-violence and violence. But thereafter, there is no such conflict. Most of the characters are violent who only believe in using violence against violence. All the major characters like Debidayal, Basu, Shafi, Hafiz only believe in violent actions of 'eye for an eye' and 'tooth for a tooth.' Even Sundari, the central female character does not hesitate in killing Shafi Usman who tries to take her with him in exchange of Mumtaz, who was taken away by her brother, Debidayal. She sits on Shafi's back and strikes his head with Shiva's idol again and again until his head is cracked open:

> Shafi was wriggling on the floor, shielding his head with his hands, and Sundary stood above him, the Shiva from the Little House in her hands. Even as he was looking, he saw her bringing it down on Shafi's head, and then, when the man rolled forward and lay limp on the carpet, he saw her bring it down again and again, as though killing a scorpion or spider, crashing in the dead man's skull until it cracked open and blood and brains spurted out in a red white mess (390).

In *A Bend in the Ganges,* Malgonkar has also shown 'self-consuming nature of violence. (Rajgopalachari, 65) through the deaths of Debidayal and Shafi Usman—the worshippers of violence. Debidayal is killed in Hindu-Muslim conflict and Shafi is killed by Sundary in an attempt of taking her away with him. Gian Talwar, basically a non-violent, and Sundari survive in the end. Through the survival of Gian and Sundari, both the killers, Malgonkar, consciously or unconsciously puts yet another question mark on the self-consuming nature of violence.

Shafi's death at the hands of Sundari, to some extent, may be justified as she killed him to save her chastity or perhaps life. But the death of Vishnudutt by Gian, basically a non-violent, is the result of later's deliberate attempt to take revenge of Hari's death.

But, Malgonkar, as a matter of fact, has proved the fears of Gandhiji about the mass destruction as a sequel of violence to be true through Hindu-Muslim riots. He has also underlined the historical fact that violence only breeds violence. If we look at the novel from this point of view, then, in a way, it is not the refutation of Mahatma's ideology of non-violence.

WORKS CITED

Iyengar, K.R., Srinivasa, *Indian Writing in English:* Delhi: Sterling Publishers Pvt. Ltd.

Malgonkar, Manohar, *A Bend in the Ganges:* London: Pan Books Ltd.

Rajgopalachari, M., *The Novels of Manohar Malgonkar:* Delhi: Prestige.

7

FEMINIST PERSPECTIVES IN SHASHI DESHPANDE'S *THAT LONG SILENCE*

L.M. JOSHI

Sashi Deshpande is a good storyteller with a talent for creating the desired mood and shaping the characters as the situation demands. *That Long Silence,* which won her the Sahitya Akademi Award for 1990, tells the story of an Indian housewife who maintained her silence throughout her life despite the hardships that threatened to break it. This novel, is the first of Deshpande's novels to be published abroad. The theme of the novel is simple. Jaya, the heroine of the novel, recalls her married life with nostalgia. She was married to Mohan. She lived with him at different places till he left her to clear himself of the charges of business malpractice. She bore him two children and the third one was aborted. She recalled her relationship with innumerable relatives and friends with compassion and understanding. She tried to come to terms with herself trying to write for herself and her family. She was determined to break her long silence. The novel ends with the return of her son Rahul, the promise of Mohan 'to return' on Friday morning and learning the truth that 'Life has always to be made possible.'

Jaya, the heroine wants to write in detail about her life:

> For, I'm not writing of all those innocent girls I've written till now; girls who ultimately mated themselves with the right men. Nor I am writing a story of a callous, insensitive husband and a sensitive suffering wife. I'm writing of us. Of Mohan and me. And I know this; you can never be the heroine of your own story. Self-revelation is a cruel story.

> The real picture, that real 'you' never emerges. Looking for it is as bewildering as trying to know how really look. Ten different mirrors show you ten different faces (1).

The novel *That Long Silence* is not as exemplary quest for self-discovery but it has no rancour and bitterness. The heroine after her traumatic experiences accepts that she is different from what she was, and therefore, expects to have a new relationship with her husband.

She is hopeful of attaining her family life, she passes through a plethora of self-doubts, fears, guilt, anger and silence towards articulation and affirmation Suman Shiya, while reviewing the novel observes that Jaya "Caught in an emotional eddy, endeavors to come to terms with her protean roles, while trying, albeit in vain, to rediscover her true self, which is but an ephemera...an unfulfilled wife, disappointed mother and failed writer" (*The Times of India*, 8 October 1989, 2). Somehow Jaya is not for the notion of patriarchal self. But she wants to erase the long silence and gravel with the problems of self-revelation and self-assessment. The process that brings her to this complex situation, which involves an exploration of childhood, youth and marriage, yet paradoxically, her deepest betrayal is caused by the domination of the role model of marriage. The novel reveals an intimate and domestic chronicle of subtle tyrannies suffered by women and of the pain of coming to self-knowledge or at least to the conditions, which must be fulfilled before the self-knowledge, can be attained. It is the story of personal journey and the effects of the journey, as expressed in the novel: "Two bullocks yoked together that was how I saw the two of us the day we came here, Mohan and I. Now I reject that image. It's wrong. If I think of us in that way, I've always thought there is only one life, no chance of a reprieve, no second chances. But in this life itself there are so many cross roads, so many choices" (191-192). The suffering of the heroine is brought to the fore and the cause of which is forcing her to come out of the shell, she has chosen to live in all these days.

Jaya's self confidence is rudely shaken at a time when her husband leaves without informing her and fails to return for many days. Jaya also finds fault with her mother for not preparing her well for the duties of a women's life. Jaya attributes her failure as a mother to her own mother's neglect of her. She realizes that after her marriage she would not know how to suckle her own child. She also realizes that her son is always keeping a distance from her. Since Mohan is not present, she reflects and finds that besides being a failure as a mother she has not been a good wife either. When she first came to her husband's house, she was ignorant of many things, say for instance she did not even know how to stitch a button to shirts. In the same manner when her husband had some problem, she started accusing him of indulging in corruption. Her husband says that he always stood by her but she was rejecting him for his corrupt practices. He further narrates that he was so because he wanted to provide comforts to his wife and children.

Deshpande portrays Jaya as the emerging new woman. She is very much conscious of her status and is prepared to listen to no one's advice but her own. She has built up a theory of her own that the daughter must fight if she wants to graduate in this world. In order to spite her mother, Jaya marries Mohan. Though Jaya is portrayed as the awakened woman, her courage and determination fade into that of a middle class romantic heroine, the moment she encounters reality. All her revolutionary ideals sag by the time the challenge presents itself. Here Jaya signifies the weakness of the servile mind of the service classes, though she is not a serving woman. She is the wife of a middle rank government servant, who dreams of riches through her husband's job. The whole edifice collapses the moment the job is taken away or is in danger. Jaya lacks the initial aggressiveness that comes so easily to an unrefined and uneducated woman. Moreover Jaya is heroic in ideas and perceptions only so long as she stays on the subjective grounds of church gate. All her heroism sags when she sifts to the upper floor flat at Dadar.

Now she reflects upon the ground realities from some height. She is not involved in them because life has come to a standstill for her. The upper floor-existence symbolizes the objective state as against the subjective mode at the church gate. She has now to overcome her setbacks. Her husband has to be reinstated, and only then her life will start functioning. If not, she shows no sign of recovery from the present situations.

Despite all the progressive ideas Jaya has—she is a role model of Indian married woman's mind. Her friend Kamat encourages Jaya to write and he chides her, for avoidance of life in her writing. For him she feels a love that is more than gratitude, a love which, falls outside the conventional boundaries. This breeds fear in her which impels her to run away from the place the moment she sees Kamat's dead body. Though she has heartfelt feelings for him, she avoids speaking out. Only after confronting the terms of her depths, she writes: "The loneliness of a man facing his death—is there anything like that in this World? his pain filled this room and we could both of us feel it. Mukta and I. The fellowship if pain seemed to bind us together; we were like two patients in hospital, suffering from the same disease, lying on the adjacent beds" (186).

Kamat helped Jaya much to make her, a writer. Somehow she also developed a soft corner for him. She thinks that she must not lend a helping hand to Kamat: "he tried to reach out to me in his loneliness and it had frightened me. I'm Mohan's wife, had thought, I'm only Mohan's wife, and I had run away" (186). Jaya perhaps does, her of a wife to a possible perfection, but fails as a human being. Another feature Jaya has, is that she is capable of making someone a scapegoat for her failures. For instance, she finds fault with her husband for her failure as a writer. At one stage she tells her husband that she gave up writing because of him. She says: "I had known then that it hadn't mattered to Mohan that I had written a good story, a story about a couple, a man who could not reach out to his wife except through her body. For Mohan it had mattered that people might think the couple was us. That the man was him. To Mohan, I had been no writer, only an exhibitionist" (144). Jaya does not want to irritate her husband by continuing her writing, which she thinks, might even break their married life. She says ironically "Perhaps, if Mohan had been angry, if he had shouted and raged at me, if he had forbidden me to write, perhaps I would have fought him and gone on. But he had shown me his hurt. And I had not been able to counter that. I had relinquished them instead, all those stories that had been likely to hurt Mohan, scared of jeopardizing the only career I had" (144). Jaya is not a revolutionary character but wants to be different from the regular housewife life style. Deshpande in order to bring out what type of mind Jaya has uses an apt image of a worm crawling into a hole to describe the state of Jaya, a budding writer fading into a typical Indian housewife:

> "Middle class, Bourgeoisie, Upper caste. Distanced from real life. Scared of writing Scared of failing. Oh God. I had though. I can't take any more. Even a worm has a hole it can crawl into. I had mine—as Mohan's wife, as Rahul's and Rati's Mother" (148).

Jaya's attitude towards her husband and family life made us think that her married life is a loveless one to an extent which is the main cause for her to drift away from her husband. She complains bitterly:

> "I'll tell you what's wrong. I've failed him. He expected something from me. From his wife and I've failed him. All these years I thought I was Mohan's wife; now he tells me I was never that, really. What am I going to do? What shall I do if he doesn't come back? (185) She concludes "Nothing. Nothing between us. But after his death, nothing between Mohan and me either. We lived together but there had been only emptiness between us" (185).

We learn from these statements that her husband Mohan has destroyed both the woman and the writer in Jaya. Because of his intriguing nature Jaya has a valid reason to be bitter with him. He is responsible for her misery. She recalls their relationship as wife and husband:

> Sensual memories are the coldest. They stir up nothing in you. As I thought of days, of my feelings, and then looked at the man lying beside me, nothing stirred in me. Those emotions and responses seemed to belong to two other people, not to the two of us lying here together.
>
> In any case, whatever my feeling had been then, I had never spoken of sex at all. It had been as if the experience was erased each time after it happened: it never existed in words. My only answer, 'No.'
>
> "Each time. After is was over, the same question: and My reply too. Invariably the same 'No.' First there is love, and then there's sex that was how I had imagined it to be. But

after living with Mohan I had realized that it would so easily be other way round" (95). So the seventeen years of their married life is led only on physical level in a superficial manner. It is a frustrating and depressing ordeal that Jaya has undergone. It will be a disgusting experience to live with a man who dose not love the woman the way she expected him to do. This to so. This is a common experience for many women in the contemporary society. At the same time, these women encounter a social problem, which is nothing but the brand they get from society as 'deserted Women.' Through the character of Jaya. Desphande has thus expressed the ambivalent attitude of contemporary educated women in India who can neither reconcile themselves to a new situation when their husbands ignore them and crush their ambition in life nor cast off their husbands, simply because the husband is like sheltering tree they cannot afford to live without. In a way, Jaya is a representative figure of the modern woman who resents her husband's callousness and becomes the victim of circumstances. By implication, the character of Jaya represents modern woman's—ambivalent attitude to married life.

In the final stage Jaya emerges as a person divested of all self-deceptions and artificialities that she has all along been living with. She considerably sobers herself after making certain self-discoveries about herself. Mohan's telegram from Delhi informing her that everything is fine and a changed Rahul is returning to help her as the situation demands. Now such things seem to be just information for Jaya and she is not terribly bothered about them.

The picture of the emotionally, physically and socially segregated words, for which these people attach importance, has vanished from her imagination. Mohan's wife image has no relevance for her.

She says that she is not concerned with the fragmentation of life or divided self. She has a new perception of life in which the family, including herself along with the other members of the family, are independent individuals with distinct identities. This means that she need not have imposed responsibilities in the family welfare and she faces any loss in the family with no emotional trauma. She has undoubtedly gained the moral courage and necessary resourcefulness required for having such principle. Yet she has to make life possible in the present and therefore put up with the realities of life with an awareness of certain social values, which prompts her to accept the established social values. This awareness provides her with a spiritual and emotional fulfilment in the world.

The emergence of women writers on the Indian Literary scene with radical outlook is a recent phenomenon, and they present an idealized image of a woman in their works. It is therefore imperative that these writers attempted to write from women's point of view. They projected well, the emotion and experiences of women as a wife, mother and as an individual facing psychological and sociological problems. These writers are also influenced by the Indian life and society to an extent. True to the ideals of these writers, Deshpande concerns herself with the plight of the modern Indian woman trying to understand herself and to preserve her identity as wife, mother and above all as a human being.

The writers of feminism are primarily concerned with the recognition of woman as a being, an autonomous being. They want woman to realize herself through self-analysis and determination. In *That Long Silence*, Jaya, the protagonist thinks of her past and tries to analyse herself and her station in life. Jaya stands for revolt against oppressing social customs that throttle women in our society. Through the process of reliving the past in her mind, Jaya gets the guidance for future. She decides to break her long seven years of silence and decides herself that she is no longer a passive partner of Mohan. She breaks her self-imposed prison wall of mind and chooses to remain in the family, and at the same time comes out of the confining slots allotted to her by the patriarchal society. Jaya looks for happiness and self-fulfilment within the family itself. She is confident of her individual prowess to face any situation and is hopeful of a change in Mohan's attitude and moves beyond the cultural stereotypes. As Toril Moi remarks, "The Principal objective of feminist criticism has always been political: it seeks to expose, not to perpetuate, patriarchal practices." (Sexual/Textual Polities: Feminist Literary Theory, XIV). This is what Deshpande does in her text. The important insight that the novelist imparts to us through Jaya is that women should accept their own responsibility for what they are. It is only through self analysis and self understanding they can begin to change their lives and overcome the hurdles in their way to progress. It is their battle, which they have to fight with determination and courage in order to attain what they want. The concluding lines in the novel epitomize the whole meaning of the novel as well as life: "I will have to speak, to listen, I will have to erase the silence between us.... We don't change overnight. It's possible that we may not change even over long periods of time. But we can always hope. Without that, life would be impossible. And if there is anything I know it is this: life has always to be made possibility" (192-193).

Feminist touches apart, *That Long Silence* is a typical English novel, which reveals to us the prevailing situation in the Indian social structure. Jaya, the heroine of the novel, gives us the new image of the Indian woman who now strives to stand on her own legs. The traditional suffering of women, in silence, has come to be broken with assertion, courage and determination, in order to march towards progress, for self-fulfilment and peaceful life.

WORKS CITED

That Long Silence. Delhi: Penguin Books. 1989.

Hunter College women's studies collective: Women's Realities, women's choices: An introduction to women's studies. New York: Oxford University Press, 1983.

Iyenger, Srinivasa K.R., *Indian Writing in English.* 1962. New Delhi: Sterling, 1985.

Krishnaswamy, Shantla, *The Woman in Indian Fiction in English.* New Delhi: Ashish, 1984.

Mukherjee Meenakshi, *Realign and Reality: The Novel and Society in India* Delhi: Oxford University Press, 1985.

Zinda, M.R., *Constraints and Conflicts of the Indian woman: A Study of Shashi Deshpande's Novels.* Madras, 1992.

8

SOCIO-POLITICAL CONCERNS IN BHABANI BHATTACHARYA'S *SO MANY HUNGERS*

MANJUSHA KAUSHIK

Indian writers of the 20th century had a strong fascination to deal with the changing national scenes related to the different levels as social, political, historical and economic. Politicians of that time wanted to make our country free from the hands of Britishers. But soon after this spirit touched the heart of every section of the society. So the Indian novelists could not remain untouched by the spirit of nationalism.

Many Indian writers have a deep sense of involvement to deal with the theme of contemporary history in their fiction. The novelists like K.S. Venkataramani and Khushwant Singh depict the contemporary issues like Salt Satyagarha or the theme of Partition in their works in the same way. Bhattacharya through his novels like *So Many Hungers, Music for Mohini, He Who Rides a Tiger, A Goddess Named Gold, Shadow from Ladakh* and *A Dream in Hawaii,* depicts the Indian life from 1940s to 1970s. Bhabani Bhattacharya, like Mulk Raj Aanad, Raja Rao and R.K. Narayan, grew up in British India, and was obsessed with the socio-political and economic conditions prevailing in the society. K. Venkata Reddy remarks in this context: *So Many Hungers* may, therefore, be taken as "a worthy illustration of how contemporary history can be transformed by a socially conscious artist into fiction of permanent relevance of mankind" (60).

In each one of these novels the novelist deals either with the socio-political events or the socio-historical events which are related to the future of India. In *So Many Hungers* he has effectively told the tragic pathos of the hungry man. In *Music for Mohini* he deals with the problems of country's social regeneration and conflict between modernism and traditionalism which the free India is facing today. *He Who Rides a Tiger* deals with the theme of hunger, poverty and the corruption in man and society. It makes an attack on the social reality of caste system. In *A Goddess Named Gold* Bhattacharya deals with the theme of economic freedom. It's a satire on those who always lived by the lust of Gold. *Shadow from Ladakh* tells what India needs for survival. In *A Dream in Hawaii* the novelist portrays the clash between the values of the east and of the west.

When Bhattacharya had started his writing career he was very much impressed by the theme of suffering in the writings of other novelists. So he decided to portray the plight of suffering people in his novels. The picture of hunger whatever be it causes and reasons is found in various colours in a Raja Rao's *Kanthapura,* Kamla Markandaya's *Nectar in a Sieve,* R.K. Narayan's *The Guide,* Mulk Raj Anand's *Untouchable* and Bhabhani Bhattacharya's *So Many Hungers* and *He Who Rides a Tiger* are representative picture of this new type of novels. Although the other writers have written on the theme of hunger but not in the same passion as Markandaya or Bhattacharya. Both are the finest exponents of this new type of novels. Bhattacharya and Markandaya have dealt forcefully not only with the theme of hunger but the theme of human degradation also.

Bhattacharya is a man of social commitment. He established himself as a leader of the suffering humanity. *So Many Hungers* portrays realistically the agony of the age. It shows the injustice of the Britishers and presents human drama against the dismal background of the Bengal famine. It deals with the theme of exploitation in the field of political, social and economic environment. Through his novel *So Many Hungers* he wanted to raise the voice against the crudities of that time. He believes in the depiction of reality in literature. But his realism is concerned with social issues of that time. He believes that the novel should portray the social picture of the period in which he is living. Writing novels with a social purpose became his main creed. He confesses that he has not believed in writing for the sake of writing. Purposive writing in the social and political context of India during the 1930s and 40s called for exposing the social, political and economic evils. In an interview he observes—"I hold that a novel must have a social purpose. It must place before the reader something from the society's point of view" (Joshi, 8).

Like other great novelists Bhabhani Bhattacharya is obsessed with the theme of hunger. His concerns with the theme of hunger is very clear in his entire work. Although the Bengal famine seized his mind but hunger also hunted him throughout his literary career. His writing is based upon man's hunger of food and other is disguised hunger of freedom. *So Many Hungers* his first novel, is primarily devoted to man's hunger of food as well as other urges. Every person in this novel has a different hunger. For example Rahoul's hunger is for a new and enlightened world order based on ethical values of life. Devta, the grandfather of Rahoul thinks for the welfare of the common humanity. Kunal has gone to the battle field of World War II without caring for his family. It shows the hunger of the new order in the society. Samarendra has a hunger of accumulating wealth as much as can possible. Kajoli's is hunger for the sacredness of heart. Hunger makes human beings inhuman and quite often the starving man quarrels inhumanly for a little bit of food. Hunger compels a young girl to show herself naked to man for the sake of getting food. Just as hunger of food and hunger of freedom play a dominant role in his writing in the same way *So Many Hungers* focuses on man's insatiable hunger for sex life and money too. This is proved by the life of Sir Abalabandhu. Although he has achieved in full measure the two fold blessings of wealth and honour, yet he is not satisfied. He is very much interested in indulging the sexual act with a young girl. So through the character of Abalabandhu the novelist wants to state the social evil which was very frequent in our society. So through his writing he wants to remove all the evils in the society. Social forces and inequalities had always played an important role in his writing. He said that "My chief purpose is to deal with the problems of social change," he has said, "I see fiction as a means to the end" (Shimer, 2).

The novel is divided into two parts. The first part represents the Basu's family and other with the peasant family of Kajoli. In the first part Devta, Samarendra and Rahoul play the dominant role. On the other hand Kajoli, her mother and Onu. The sad story of Kajoli represents the pathetic fate of the millions of people. They suffered a lot due to the disastrous famine of Bengal in 1943. Dorothy Shimer says in this context "So Many Hungers was written out of compulsion to bring in light the intense sufferings of people" (Shimer, 29).

So Many Hungers describes the tragic story of a man-made famine in Bengal. Due to Bangal famine the condition of the people became so miserable that it was impossible to imagine its depth to the extent man had degraded himself. "India's economic backwardness and poverty were not due to the niggardliness of nature. They were man made" (Chandra, 151). India was very rich and prosperous but due to the result of foreign rule exploitation, starvation and poverty prevailed.

The novel is related to this famous line man eats food not money. The Bengal famine of 1943 was too horrible to describe. Bhattacharya says in this regard:

> Human endurance ebbed, Hungry children cried themselves to death, streams of desperate men ventured out of their ancestral homes in search of food, hanging on to the foot boards of railway trains, riding on the sunbacked roof" (SMH, 110-111).

The novel *So Many Hungers* deals with the character of Rahoul in a new perspective. In today's time the personal profits are more important than the public interest. Everybody has his own care. But the novelist who has an humanitarian outlook, provides the same status to Rahoul. He is called the embodiment of the novelist himself. The story begins with the Character of Rahoul, who is very much anxious to hear the news of his baby cry at the same time he heard the news of the war in Europe. The novelist had a keen observation of the incidents. When Rahoul heard about war he was very much disturbed because war has two shape. If it is launched for the betterment of people, it will have a positive aspect but if it will for their own benefits, it will take the negative shape. We can compare this conception with the struggle for freedom. The freedom fighters fight for the sake of the country.

Their cause was noble because it was in the interest of the countrymen. Britishers ruled the country for their own interest. Rahoul is totally different with his elders. He does not care for his own benefits. The novelist wants to state that, if everybody is selfish who will care to look after the country. The novel must have a social purpose. He wanted to do something for the hungry humanity. Because it was the need of the day. In his blood, he feels the voice of India throb which has always been an affirmation and not negation, of life. Rahoul is convinced that suffering purifies human beings. Bhattacharya remains the essential goodness and nobility of the hungry people. The moral uprightness and unselfishness of hungry people has been described in very detail. For example Onu, a brother of Kajoli gathered a lot of figs to give to the others or the starving old mother of Kajoli is called a compassionate lady. She gives her cow to save the life of infant. Although throughout the novel we come across various instances of misery, poverty, starvation but these negative elements are subdued into the background when we think the hope and assertion of the self. The conflict of the self throughout the novel has not been with the materialistic forces of evil but with the social forces of exploitation. The novelist is successful to strike the heart of everyone.

A note of realism strikes in the account of a given situation of the famine of 1943. The famine is symbolically crucible into which both eastern and western characters are put into test. *So Many Hungers* denotes many corners of mankind which demand their fulfilment and gratification. Through the famine prism of human predicament the author portrays the various faces of human character. The famine primarily involves the sufferers facing a natural calamity in various ways. Majority of them faced it with meekness but many of them degrades themselves to a beastly level. Samarendra Basu is one of the famous example. He did not like that the famine should come to an end. The selfish people belonging to these categories do not see this horrible situation of hunger of mankind with detachment but find unique opportunity for exploiting the situation in their own self interest.

This novel reflects the image of Gandhi in Rahoul. He is very much anxious to see the new era grounded by the higher values and ideals. To him nothing is more important or valuable than the safety of the common people of the society. He works for the humanity with the true real spirit. In his voice we can hear the voice of many young excited revolutionaries. They had firm belief that their effort will not be wasted. One day they will change the established codes of life. He has his own theory. Although he has the spark of Gandhian views but not in the same way as we can find in Bakka and Lalu in Anand's *Untouchable* or Moorthy in *Kanthapura*. He is a scientist by profession. In him Bhattacharya presents a western educated Indian intellectual under the influence of Gandhian ideas. In this context Devta tells Rahoul.

> I am proud of my people. They are not bright and knowing and civilized, like you city breds, but they are good people. Centuries of hardships could not shake their faith in human values (SMH, 24).

One thing we can get from this novel is that the novelist is not against the British people, he is against their policy. Through the mouth of Devta, he tried to say that there is distinction between the British rule and the British people. Devta describes it in this way:

> Why should you fight the people of England? They are good people. The people are good everywhere. Our fight is with the rulers of England who hold us in subjection for their narrow interest (SMH, 21).

What was the reason that Indians were very much against the British people. The answer is inhumanity of the rulers towards them. British policy was responsible for it. "The Indian National Movement even it's early days had increasingly make a large number of people conscious of the evils of the foreign domination and fastening the feeling of patriotism in the masses. Secondly the Britishers were not ready to accept any demand for reforms of Indians" (Bhattacharya Glimpses, 225).

Through his novel *So Many Hungers* he wanted to give a lesson to the people that social and political reform cannot be possible by the efforts of one or two persons. It can be achieved by the joint efforts of so many persons one after another like Vivekananda, Raja Ram Mohan Roy, Gandhi, Nehru, Dayananda, Shradhananda etc. The novelist was also the product of that time. "The major impact of national awakening in the 19th century was also seen in the field of social reforms" (Chandra, 18).

Through the character of Kajoli who is the heroine of the novel he wants to say that sacredness of heart is also the quality of freedom loving persons. She is an innocent girl. She enjoys a very short span of time with Kishore. When she was forced to join the pimp but she tried a lot to save herself at any cost. Through Kajoli the novelist presents a rustic girl who has a spirit of freedom. She is an incarnation of faith in the nobleness and fullness of life. She has inherited the fundamental values and manners of India. Although she suffered a lot but not ready to sacrifice herself. It's a strength of her character. Such boldness is very much necessary to break the chain of slavery because God sends miseries to the people only to test their real character. So don't betray yourself, have faith and courage.

Bhabani's vision in *So Many Hungers* is a positive one. He is like a social reformer who believes that there should be a fusion of ethical values in literature. "*So Many Hungers* is thus an allegory of the victory of human values over the sordid and vicious ways of life. It is an allegory of the assertion of invincible spirit of India over the sinister power of the alien imperialists" (Raizada, 85).

The novelist is an idealist. He dreams for a bright future of India and Indians. We can find the smell of positivity in his novel. The main purpose to write this novel is the victory of the human spirit over the strong power of the Britishers as well as the selfish Indians. This novel leads to the path of affirmation not negation. Suffering does not snatch away the values which they cherish high. His major concern has been to focus on the major historical crisis, shaking the destiny of the nation. Political freedom is not only a cry from one's mouth but also a cry for freedom from all types of evils and exploitation. The novelist gives the lesson of nobleness and goodness to people. Ethical values have their own place in the lives of the people. The novelist has a firm belief that if a man has not done any wrong in his life, definitely he will get success and present a true example to the coming generation.

In this novel Bhattacharya made an attempt to arouse the conscience of the people of India to stand against injustice and tyranny adopted by Britishers. And to some extent he achieved success in his efforts.

REFERENCES

Bhattacharya Bhabani, *Glimpses of Indian History*, New Delhi: Sterling Publishers Private Limited, 1980. *So Many Hungers*, New Delhi: Orient Paperbacks, 1978.

Chandra, Bipin, *Modern India*, New Delhi: National Council of Educational Research and Training, 1990.

Joshi, Sudhakar, *An Evening with Bhabani, The Sunday Standard*, April 27, 1969.

Raizada, Harish, *Fiction As Allegory*, Novels of Bhabani Bhattacharya in *Perspectives on Bhabani Bhattacharya*. Ramesh K. Srivastav, Ghaziabad, Nirmal Prakashan, 1982.

Reddy K. Venkata, *Major Indian Novelists*, New Delhi: Prestige Books, 1990.

Sorot, Balram S., *The Novels of Bhabani Bhattacharya*, New Delhi: Prestige Books, 1991.

Srivastav, Ramesh K., *Perspectives on Bhabani Bhattacharya*, Ghaziabad: Vimal Prakashan, 1982.

Shimer, Dorothy Blair, *Bhabani Bhattacharya*, Boston: Twayne Publishers, 1975.

9

READABILITY OF *DIFFICULT DAUGHTERS*

MANJU ROY

Manju Kapur's debut novel, *Difficult Daughters,* was published in 1998 and it has been winning several accolades since then. It was short-listed for the Crossword Book Award in India and also earned the prestigious 1999 Commonwealth Writer's Prize for the Best First Book category in the Eurasia region. Meenakshi Mukherjee has hailed *Difficult Daughters* as 'an impressive novel,' Shirley Kossick appreciates it as 'a part of the new and vital wave of Anglo-Indian fiction,' Bibi Shah finds it 'an eye opener in many ways' and Nira Gupta-Casale discovers it as 'a novel about female desire and entrapment, about compromise and compliance....' Various aspects of the novel have been researched on but, surprisingly, readability of the novel has not been taken up seriously. While reviewing the novel some critics have found it quite readable. For instance, Nira Gupta-Casale considers it 'an extremely readable novel.' When an informal survey was done, several university teachers working in the area of Indian Writing in English confirmed Gupta-Casale's opinion intuitively. As no one, it seems, has taken pains to assess the reasons for its high readability, this paper, therefore, is a modest attempt to explore the factors responsible for the novel's very high readability.

Readability of a text is normally decided on the basis of some mathematical calculation or by using word-processing software. There are several popular readability tests like Gunning Fog Test and Flesch Readability Test ("Readability Tests," 1). Gunning Fog Test takes into account the number of words in a paragraph, the number of sentences in the paragraph and the number of words having three and more syllables. This test implies that short sentences written in plain English achieve a better score than long sentences written in complicated language. Flesch Readability Test measures readability by taking the number of words in an average sentence and the number of syllables in an average word. In this test the higher the score, the easier the text is to understand. So, a score of hundred implies that the text is very easy to understand and a score of zero means that the text is extremely difficult to read. However, in this article the readability has been considered in a somewhat non-technical sense. Here it has been associated with the lucidity and flow of the text and the ease one experiences in reading the novel.

One of the sources of high readability of the novel appears to lie in the extensive use of Hindi and Punjabi words in the novel. These words have been derived from different areas of experience. In fact, the English used by Manju Kapur is geared towards expressing a distinctly Indian sensibility. Therefore, her English has definitely a local flavour. This variety of English (*i.e.* Indian English) may be frowned at by purists but one finds its excellent defence in Kamala Das's 'An Introduction' to *The Old Playhouse and Other Poems*:

> The language I speak
> Becomes mine, its distortions, its queerness
> All mine, mine alone. It is half English, half
> Indian, funny perhaps, but it is honest,
> It is as human as I am human, don't
> You see? It voices my joys, my longings, my
> Hopes, and it is as useful to me as cawing
> Is to crows or roaring to the lions, it
> Is human speech, the speech of the mind that is
> Here and not there, a mind that sees and hears and
> Is aware...
>
> (*quoted in Nihalani*, 29)

Manju Kapur voices her joys and hopes by using rich and colourful expressions of colloquial Punjabi and creates the cultural context of her plot. An example of this creation is evident in 'the devotion with which the native Punjabi extols the soul satisfying virtues of butter and lassi' (Gupta-Casale).

The milk had a thick layer of *malai*, yellow, not white, like nowadays. And when food was cooked, ah, the fragrance of *ghee*! At this point, words fail them.

I had grown up on the mythology of pure ghee, milk, butter, and *lassi*, and whenever, I came to Amritsar, I noticed the fanatical gleam in the eyes of people as they talked of those legendary items. Perhaps, if I could have shared that passion, the barriers of time and space would have melted like pure ghee in the warmth of my palm (4).

The source of high readability can also be traced to the novelist's use of code-switching devices. Code switching is normally defined as the use of more than one language in the execution of a speech-act. She uses this device at the lexical and syntactical levels, usually noun phrases, to express herself in a better and satisfying way. Her use of this device seems to be governed sometimes by the non-availability of an equivalent word in English and at other times by a mere choice to make the context or narration more realistic. In the sentence, "A

Table 9.1: Nouns

Food	Place	Profession	Event	Relation	Dress	Utensils	Miscellaneous
Atta	Ghat	Chowkidar	Chauth	Bhai Saheb	Pyjama	Thali	Sandhya
Malai	Angan	Pundit	Uthala	Bua	Kurta	Katori	Havan
Lassi	Gully	Randi	Shaddi	Maji	Kameez	Karahi	Durries
Puris	Kothi	Dhobi		Chachi	Dhoti	Patila	Furlong
Luchis	Dhara-mshala	Munshi		Bade Pitaji	Dupatta		Lauki
Kulchas	Zenana Aangan	Bania		Baoji			Baithak
Tandoori				Bhai			Kewara
Morraba				Beta			
Sherbat				Masi			
Papad				Pitaji			
Dal				Bhenji			
Pakora							
Chutney							
Khas							
Dahi							
Paneer							
Mathri							

woman's shaan is in her home" (13), Kapur's choice of '*shaan*' instead of 'pride' lends this expression a homely and realistic touch. Her use of Hindi/Punjabi words represents a vast area of experiences, but it is remarkable that the words are mostly concrete ones as opposed to abstract ones. Here concrete words refer to the objects normally perceived by our sense organs. A list of these words used by Kapur, shown in Table 9.1 not only refers to a wide spectrum of her experiences but also shows that she is trying to make all the details of the novel realistic, thus increasing readability.

Table 9.2: Other Words

Reduplication	Religious Invocation	Adjective	Exclamation	Compound Word
Seedha-saadha	Allah-o-Akbar	Shaan	Bap re	Puris and parathas
Shor-shaar	Har, har Mahadev	Gandi	Arre	Zenana angan
Bas-bas	Bole so Nihal	Badmash	He Bhagwan	Gajjar-mooli
			Hai re, hai re	Dhoti kurta jooti
			Arre wah	

Table 9.2 given above suggests that Manju Kapur switches code on various levels like reduplications, religious invocations, exclamations and compounding. Further, she uses this device in expressing agreement, affirmation and consent. The following extracts illustrate this point:

> 'What a lovely place to be finally laid to rest!'
> '*Hoon*,' said Virmati absently who saw nothing so remarkable about the gravestones (176).
>
> At the doorway she (Kasturi) turned back once to say, 'Indu,...use the fresh butter in the doli, the old one is for ghee.'
> '*Han*,' said Indu... (74).

Kapur extends the use of this code-switching device to phrases also and forms the expressions like,

> '*puris and parathas* wrapped in Britannia-bread waxed paper' (02),
> '*aalu ki sabzi* in *mithai* boxes' (2),
> 'They...skirted the *zenana angan*' (180),
> '...and pull her *sari palla*' (213).

Readability is also caused by the narrative technique used in the text. The major part of the story is narrated by the author herself, who seems to be omnipresent and does not take part in the story. This type of narrator is called 'heterodiegetic' (Genette, 255-6). Only a very small part is narrated by Ida, Virmati's daughter, who is a participant also. A narrator of this type is labelled as 'homodigetic' (Genette, 255-6). Ida starts narrating the tale with a very cryptic statement: "The one thing I had wanted was not to be like my mother." (1) And from this very point readers get curious 'to explore, and analyse why she did not like to be like her mother and relate the answer to the larger issue of patriarchy' (Bala and Chandra). And the book ends, as it began, with the angry Ida's comment:

> This book weaves a connection between my mother and me, each word a brick in a mansion I made with my head and my heart. Now live in it, Mama and leave me be. Do not haunt me any more (259).

In this way, the novel appears to form a complete circle and this circularity gives a direction, continuity and speed to readers. Ida takes over the narration of the tale at different points in the novel, but only for a very brief period and this breaks the monotony in the reading of the novel. Ida starts the story in Chapter 1 wherein she talks about her dead mother just after her funeral at Delhi and then she reaches Amritsar where she starts piecing together her dead mother's past, but as she has been able to provide only a small aspect of her life, we get the remaining big part of the story mainly by the author. Ida takes up the job of a narrator again in Chapter 9. She, along with Kailashnath, goes to the college where her father worked for a very long time and her mother's love affair bloomed with Harish. Thereafter, she again starts telling the story in Chapter 17 (second part) wherein she meets Swarana Lata Sondhi, the roommate of Virmati during her Lahore days, to explore some more facets of her mother's personality. Later, she again tries to reconstruct the story in Chapter 19 (second part). Here, she comes to know how Swarana Lata helps her mother to get rid of the unwanted pregnancy. Further, in chapter 23 (second part) Ida talks to her Masi about her mother's marriage and in Chapter 25, she is trying to pick up the loose threads of her mother's marital life. And finally, at the end of the Epilogue, she becomes autobiographical and bids farewell to her mother's memory.

The reader develops a bond of trust with the author who is the main narrator in the novel. Her omniscience can be felt by her presence as a storyteller in about 250 pages of the novel, which runs into 259 pages. This is also realized by her familiarity with the characters' innermost thoughts and feelings, her knowledge of past and present and her presence in locations where characters meet in total privacy. In addition, what makes this novel compelling reading and distinguishes it from other tales of adulterous love and romantic intrigue is the sympathy and integrity with which the author and Ida reconstruct the past of Virmati (Gupta-Casale).

Mukul Kesavan, a famous novelist, commends *Difficult Daughters* as 'a first rate realistic novel' (Bala and Chandra, 106). A close analysis of the novel reveals that realism also promotes a high degree of reliability, and realism, to a large extent, is realized in 'verisimilitude' and 'credibility.' Cassirer defines art as 'a continuous process of concretion' (144). Leech and Short explain this definition in the following way: 'The sense of being in the presence of actual individual things, events, people, and places, is the common experience we expect to find in literature' (156) and this very aspect of the illusion of reality is called verisimilitude. The novel is full of instances where readers get the impression of being participants or observers themselves. For example, Virmati's traumatic experience of unwanted pregnancy mitigates the gap between a reader and a participant, at least for a short while:

> Quickly she calculated dates.... She was certain she was pregnant. With this certainty, the nausea came again, ripping through her throat, salivating her tongue. She thought of all the hours she had spent over her practical files, her teaching charts,... What would happen to her BT now? (141).

Verisimilitude is closely connected with another aspect of realism called credibility. Credibility is "likelihood or believability of the fiction as a 'potential reality'..." (Leech and Short, 157). Kasturi gets surprised at the fuss that people are making in the house after Virmati fails at her FA examination. She does not give importance to the success in the examination—instead, she strongly believes: "...it is the duty of every girl to get married" (13). Her belief lends credibility to the novel because the same belief was a part of Indian consciousness till some years ago.

A lot of colloquial expressions also make the novel lucid. Some examples are quoted below:

> Hai re, beti! (13).
>
> He is ill, he is sick, he has fainted, *hai re, hai re.* (78).
>
> Come here beta (202).
>
> Mornings, toast and milk. Lunch dal, rice, chappati, vegetable, dahi, sometimes a sweet dish, for tea, pakora or mathri, for dinner, dal, sabzi, sometimes with paneer, rice, chapatti (108).

In summing up, we may say that the novel is brilliant not only because it is 'about female desire and entrapment, about compromise and compliance' (Gupta-Casalc) but also because of its high readability which is triggered by Kapur's unique handling of the English language marked by an abundance of Hindi and Punjabi words and by her use of code switching devices and several colloquial expressions. In addition, Kapur's narrative technique and her sincere effort to make the novel realistic also enhance the readability of the text.

WORKS CITIED

Bala, S. and Subhash Chandra, Manju Kapur's *Difficult Daughter*: An Absorbing Tale of Fact and Fiction. *50 years of Indian Writing.* Ed. by R.K. Dhawan. New Delhi: Indian Association for English Studies. Year not mentioned.

Cassirer, Ernest, *An Essay on Man*. New Haven, Conn: Yale University Press. 1944.

Genette, G., *Figures III.* Paris: Seuil. 1972.

Gupta-Casale, Nira. Date and Year not mentioned. Online posting. Accessed 28 November 2000. http://www.cohums.ohio-state.edu/comp/bulletin/nira.html

Kossick, Shirley. 1998. Review *of Difficult Daughters.* Online posting. Accessed 23 October 2000. http://www.mg.co.za/mg/books/9809/980907-newfiction.html

Leech, G. and M. Short, *Style in Fiction.* London: Longman. 1987.

Mukherjee, M., 1998. What caught the eye. *The Hindu.* 20 December 1998.

Nihalani, N.K. 1985, English in the Third World: Changing Attitudes. *The Journal of Indian Writing in English.* January 1985. Vol. 13, No. 1.

"Readability Tests." On line posting. Accessed 11 November 2002. http://members.austarmetro.com.au/~quasar/usability-readabilty.html

Shah, Bibi. 1999, An Eye opener. Online posting. Accessed 7 November 2000. http://www.shop.barnesanfnoble.com/bookSearch

10

MANOJ DAS'S *CYCLONES*: AN AUTHENTIC INDIAN NOVEL

H.P. SHUKLA

> The spiritual, the infinite is near and real and the gods are real and the worlds beyond not so much beyond as immanent in our own existence. That which to the western mind is myth and imagination is here an actuality and a strand of the life of our inner being, what is there beautiful poetic idea and philosophic speculation is here a thing constantly realised and present to the experience.
>
> The dominant note in the Indian mind, the temperament that has been at the foundation of all its culture ... philosophy, religion, art and life has been, I have insisted, spiritual, intuitive and psychic.
>
> India can best develop herself and serve humanity by being herself and following the law of her own nature.
>
> (Sri Aurobindo 268, 307, 432)

I

A novel is generally about a group of people placed in a set of circumstances brought about by life's mysterious ways, and a vantage point, either revealing an infinity of life's contours or else parading a false perspective of the brain's manufacture, from which the nature of human existence is viewed. But more important than the parts is the vision of the Whole and the resultant insight and understanding it affords into that mysterious affair called Life. If there is something essentially unique about the Indian way of life, it must lead to the possibility of a manner of fictional writing which can be characteristically called Indian. This paper attempts first to explore the question of Indianness and then to show how Manoj Das's *Cyclones*, in all the above-mentioned aspects, is an authentic Indian novel.

Contemporary Indian English Writing, especially Fiction, seems to be heading towards a dangerous fjord where it must face the Sphinx and answer a few serious questions. Long back in 1972, Mulk Raj Anand noted "a tendency in Indian-English writing to please the publishers in the West and to win popularity by pandering to Anglo-American predilections about India" (41). Following an inevitable curve, in the year 2000, Shauna Singh Baldwin asserts, "We are the third generation of Indians writing in English. The first were writers like R.K. Narayan.... We are truly diaspora writers because though I had a spell of schooling in India, I have never held an Indian passport" (qtd. in Verma 1). By what stretch of imagination can such a writer be placed in the tradition of Narayan and Raja Rao, leave alone the great immemorial Indian tradition? Rao, incidentally, defined his credo in no uncertain terms: "One has to convey in a language that is not one's own the spirit that is one's own" (qtd. in Anand 25). Obviously, Rao meant by 'one's own' the Indian and not the Indo-American spirit. Can a tradition be inherited through chromosomes alone, or does it impose an imperative necessity of mingling with its people and breathing its air? It is by a continuous confrontation at every moment with the values and insights of a culture and its people that one matures into its soil and inherits the tradition.

Ronald Nixon, an Englishman, once warned Dilip Kumar Roy: "Europe never forgets, Dilip, that bread is necessary; only she forgets, too easily, that man does not live by bread alone. But you, as a Hindu, should not adopt the European as your Guru for showing you the way, since it has been shown you by your own great ancestors long ago" (Roy, *Yogi* 7). Unfortunately, the Indian diaspora in the process of acquiring the English language got unwittingly burdened with a borrowed, artificial and cloned Western psyche—the European guru. Far from being rooted in the essential Indian matrix, they represent the sensibility of a dispossessed and uprooted race, a race floating in a no-man's-land, neither Indian nor Western. When you read Hardy, you love him because he is authentically English, rooted in his soil, and rooted therefore in our earth; or you love Premchand because he too has a vision that springs directly from the earth. But much of what passes today as modern or contemporary Indian English fiction is rooted in the mid-air planes. Not that we do not empathize with the joys and sufferings of Trishuncou and his children, but we shall of necessity keep them on the margin, for they do not bring sustenance to our soul. Many of these writers seeking an alien law of perception lost or abandoned their soul in the process. The soulless race has our compassion, not our obeisance. It is not for nothing that Krishna admonishes twice, word by word, in the Gita: *shreyaanswadharmo vigunah pardharmatswanusthitat*—"Better is one's own law of works, *svadharma,* though in itself faulty than an alien law well wrought out" (III, 35; XVIII, 47).

Indian critics, no doubt, will have to concede a corner, if not the mainstream, to the diaspora writing. But before doing that, they have to free themselves from the fetters of a colonial intellectual culture and win back the true Indian mind in its pristine purity and splendour. Jussawalla's remark that "Indian literary critics are generally highly subjective, ill-read and contentious and wouldn't be tolerated for a moment in the West" (25) may contain a grain of truth but needs to be corrected and put into its place. As for subjectivity, Indians inherited it living and throbbing in their blood long before A.N. Whitehead declared, "Apart from the experiences of the subjects there is nothing, nothing, bare nothingness" (*Process and Reality*, qtd. in Prem 14). For being ill-read, it is really unfortunate that not all of us could have had our education abroad. In a country where most universities do not have even a tolerable library, and one can mange a first-class degree by reading third-class 'notes,' being 'ill-read' seems, for the present, an unavoidable condition for many, if not all, of us. What are we to do in such a situation? Listen again to Raja Rao, "One has to convey in a language that is not one's own the spirit that is one's own," and take courage from the fact that scholarship is neither essential to gain, nor does it warrant, an insight into life and truth. Finally, we do not write for a 'standing' in the West, but to win back a truth and insight that springs from our own soil. We shall acknowledge all that is great in Man's discovery in any place and time, but an ancient vision must refuse to be led by the gropings of an upstart.

But what constitutes that essential Indianness for which we have been arguing? Is it a set of behavioural responses, beliefs and knowledge, or a *shraddha,* a living faith and vision, from which all these spring? One insight of this *shraddha* that lies at the core of all others is that nothing is done or undertaken here in this land, except by the souls deluded in ignorance, for its own sake but for the sake of Divine: even the wife and children, says the Upanishad, are dear not for themselves but for the Brahman. No great Indian writing was ever done for the sake of writing, or for a Booker, but for the sole sake of revealing and bringing out in concrete symbols the domains of the highest Truth. Not only have those who composed the Veda and the Upanishads, but also the great poets of later generations been votaries of Truth. Poetry was always a by-product and never the chief occupation. And what great poems of marvellous excellence! From the Veda down to the great Shankaracharya, Tagore and Sri Aurobindo the highest truth has always outpoured itself in massive structures of reverberating poems. Indian Philosophy, which is *darshanam*—a seeing—and no mere cogitation, found its way to people's hearts through poetry and other forms of literature and seldom through its prose treatises. Truth alone, nothing else, has always been and must remain the foundation of Indian literature and all other arts. How is it that the great paintings, sculptures and architectural monuments in this country, revealing in their exposition of Truth, never bear the name of their artists? The little self, the great individual of the West, has no place in this land unless fully subservient to that great Self, the Mahat Atman.

In his introduction to an anthology of contemporary Indian writing (1974) Adil Jussawalla quotes an English critic saying that India "is the sub-continent of wisdom, love, poverty and overcrowding" and then goes on to comment,

> Nothing in this anthology suggests that India is a land of 'wisdom' and 'love.' 'Poverty' and 'overcrowding,' the other

> two factors in Mr. Connolly's description, fatally out weight (sic) the first two in the contemporary Indian writer's experience and this anthology inevitably reflects this (17-18).

Writing in 1987, Manoj Das in his *Cyclones* proves that, ironically, it is the English critic who is nearer the mark than his Indian counterpart. The essence of Indianness lies in its inimitable way of approaching and apprehending the Reality. And there is only this Way that alone is Real: the external objective reality per se, as modern theories of language and knowledge also attest, remains unknown and ungraspable:

> But what are concepts save formulations and creations of thought, which, instead of giving us the true forms of objects, show us rather the forms of thought itself? ...The question as to what reality is apart from these forms, and what are its independent attributes, becomes irrelevant here. For the mind, only that can be visible which has its source in some peculiar way of seeing, some intellectual formulation and intuition of meaning (Ernst Cassirer 112-113).

The so-called reality is therefore defined by the lens, the eye that looks at it. For the man armed with an economic lens of a capitalistic society it is the poverty and overcrowding of India that looms large. For a native who has grown from her immemorial roots India at her core is the land of Krishna's flute and Buddha's compassion. A serious and mature Indian mind—though aware of and fairly concerned sometime with the peripheral issues in time: poverty, corruption or dowry-deaths—seeks always the timeless dimensions of its land.

It is in this sense that Manoj Das can rightly be introduced as a quintessential Indian English novelist. In a tribute to Das, Bhavan's Journal noted: "Here is a writer truly Indian in his vision and wisdom and truly universal in his appeal" (qtd. in Raja 99). His fiction, like that of Raja Rao and R.K. Narayan, brings out the essential Indian spirit. It is macabre, mysterious, mythological and occult. It is also dream-like, as if woven by *Maya*. An Indian persona has a different and distinct pair of eyes. He has a consciousness, formed or floating in the collective matrix, rising to the surface or hidden in the subliminal, which looks at reality as an ever-living complexity of a variegated whole. It is an apprehension of Krishna's Universal Form which includes all the gods, poets, Rishis, planes of being, life, matter, counter view-points, denials, *asuras*, and all else that can be imagined. It is so different from the contemporary Western view-point which is dry, objective, scientific, rational, or else, hallucinatory and fantastical, a ghost without any life in it. In Manoj Das we truly come close to a ghost which is life itself, or the Holy Ghost, shall we say! His is an extraordinary sensibility that can sensuously apprehend the eerie and supernatural darkness of Indian villages and the primordial Indian sense and awareness. He is an Indian English writer who is through and through an Indian and has a thorough grasp of the English language. "What is Manoj Das? A social commentator? A psychiatrist? A sly peeper into people's hearts? Or just a plain storyteller?" asks M.V. Kamath and then neatly sums up his response: "Manoj Das is all these, and an incorrigible Indian besides" (qtd. in the blurb, Manoj Das, *Farewell to a Ghost*).

II

Manoj Das's forte is the short story and his first collection in English, *A Song for Sunday and Other Stories*, appeared in 1967. In Oriya, his mother tongue, however, Das had published his first volume of poems at the age of fifteen in 1949, and the first collection of short stories two years later in 1951. Since then, he has published nine collections of short stories in English, and ten in Oriya. In 1972, he received the prestigious Sahitya Akademi Award for his short stories. He also received the Orissa Sahitya Akademi Award twice in 1965 and 1989.

In 1987, when Manoj Das published his first novel, *Cyclones*, he was already a well established and fairly mature writer. Prof. Shiv K. Kumar's remark that "*Cyclones* appears to be a novel steeped in poetic vision" (qtd. in Raja 58) clearly suggests the depth and richness of this work. But as the book remains rather little known in academic circles, it would be helpful to have a brief synopsis of the plot, bearing in mind that a synopsis in its selection is also an interpretation.

By sheer accident of birth and fate Sudhir as a young child finds himself transplanted to the decaying feudal house of the Chowdhuries of Kusumpur. As he grows he comes to love the place and its natural surroundings, but the unknown details of his birth keep returning with an ever-increasing torment and humiliation even long after his formal adoption by his surrogate father, Hari Chowdhury. Hence, when he is forced to move to the town for his studies and gets passionately involved in the freedom movement, he does not show any desire to return to the village. But the sudden mysterious disappearance of Hari Chowdhury compels him back to Kusumpur. A near-total devastation of the village caused by an unprecedented cyclone impels him to participate in the suffering and loss of man, bird and beast.

The English Sahibs have recently arrived in Kusumpur to build an airstrip and port as part of their war preparation. The village elders are bewildered by the Sahib's strange culture making inroads in their ancient life, when arrives a new threat to their innocence from a group of five relief-workers from 'foreign' lands where women dress like men. Among them is Shyam, a self-seeking misdirected young man of leftist ideology, who has come to build a mass-base for his revolutionary movement. Others have come as members of some fancy welfare society. Reena, the secretary, is a rich man's daughter who has retained her innocence and has a distinct romantic flair for life. She impulsively falls in love with the dreamy natural ambience of Kusumpur and returns a richer and changed person. Shyam stays on stirring the neglected and unwanted elements in the village. Brindavan, the faithful manager of the Chowdhuries, dies and with him comes the end of an age. Ravi, his grandson, while taking over the mantle inherits the burden of a tradition.

Kamal uses his sister Reena to get Sudhir invited for her birthday party where he fools a naive Sudhir to acquire a fifty-acre plot in Kusumpur. Seth Mukund Das. Reena's father, is an industrialist and freedom-fighter. The town, which is deliberately left unnamed to suggest its universality, breeds people who are corrupt, ambitious, self-seeking, and through and through hypocrites. It is also the local centre of national politics. Reena, it is obvious, has romantically fallen for Sudhir.

A growing crisis back home forces Sudhir to return. The British government have decided to close the village river,

Kheya, as part of their developmental project for the airstrip and port. For Shyam this is a godsend opportunity to organise the villagers into a powerful tool of agitation; for Sudhir it is a painful death of his roots. In an unguarded angry moment, Sudhir threatens to behead the contractor responsible for the construction work on the Kheya. And lo! the contractor is beheaded. Sudhir is the obvious suspect and is forced to take refuge in the forest hermitage of Soumyadev.

The hermitage proves a place of illumination, discovery and experience and for the first time in his life Sudhir is at peace with himself and the world. When, on hearing from Ravi, Reena arrives to take Sudhir away to the town, he refuses to leave his newly-found sanctuary. But circumstances once again—this time, the last wish of a dying woman, Brindavan's wife—make him return to Kusumpur. The woman, just before she dies, reveals that Sudhir is Brindavan's son from his youthful amorous misadventure. Sudhir could have gone back to the hermitage but for his discovery of an impending catastrophe of Hindu-Muslim riots in Kusumpur. A heroic courage taking over him at the spur of the moment averts the crisis, but he is taken into the police custody for the contractor's murder.

He is acquitted by the court only to find the whole nation engulfed in the dark night of terror, suspicion and hatred. Almost in a daze, he finds himself travelling towards the city when he befriends Haru Mia, an equally lost and bewildered soul from the other community. As the two companions wander through the maze of horror and genocide, the reader is left benumbed at the inexplicable madness of humanity. It is a virtual hell burning everywhere and devouring with a demoniac laughter the senses, mind and heart. Sudhir's chance encounter with Lily/Lalita, a sex-worker in a brothel, provides him ironically with a rare oasis of love in an otherwise vast desert of inhumanity. Haru Mia falls victim to rioters and Sudhir lands up in jail. Rescued from there by Seth Mukund Das, now a political big-gun, Sudhir finds himself hailed as a freedom fighter and is nominated for the coming assembly elections. In another heroic act in the last scene he saves the situation both for a reluctant acrobat who refuses to perform and for the village folk who have gathered to watch that performance. At the end of a seemingly unending nightmare, Sudhir is able to recapture the face of Soumyadev, "the face of his own peace" and "waited for the sunrise to lead his steps" (*Cyclones* 183).[1]

III

A note appended at the beginning, possibly by the author himself, offers a very good introduction to the novel:

> This is the story of an Indian village and of characters caught in the current of a historic transition. The period is 1944-46, the eve of India's independence. The centre of the setting is a ruined feudal house.
>
> The experiences and disillusionments the protagonist goes through reflect the socio-psychological order and disorder that mark this phase of time; at a more significant level, they also reflect the inevitable process of his inner life and growth.

But *Cyclones*, though woven around Sudhir Chowdhury, the young protagonist, is not about him; more important though than him are Kusumpur and its people, it is not about them either. Sudhir and Kusumpur are miniature figurines that symbolise a contemporary and also an eternal facet of India. In quite a strange manner the novel reveals the intersection of time and eternity. Set against the historical backdrop of Partition, it portrays an accurate picture of the changes taking place and yet escapes from getting trapped in a time-flux. Its own envisioning of characters and their perception of reality is from a point where, to borrow Eliot's phrase, 'all time is eternally present.' Amid all the superficial turbulence of change, seated in a centre of calm, shines the gentle, powerful and unobtrusive light of a mystic Soumyadev which at the end of the day points towards an ever-present dawn of illumination.

There is only a single occurrence of a natural cyclone in the novel but the plural title forces us to look for some more, equally devastating and at planes other than obvious and natural. There is one that threatens to demolish the age-old socio-economic and cultural fabric of Kusumpur; another of a greater magnitude is out to swallow the very soul and self of a great nation; and yet another that rages silently, destroying and regenerating Shiva-like, in multiple vortices at the psychic centre of the young protagonist. But behind it all pervades a secret undisturbed calm of the universal Spirit.

The star-lit canvas, for there are no bright burning torches in the middle, stands mapped out in four distinct zones: Kusumpur, the town, the city (both unnamed), and equidistant from all three at the centre, the hermitage of Soumyadev. This is the ground which fosters and informs Sudhir Chowdhury and then throws him out to decipher a meaning in the senseless whirl emanating from the heart of darkness to envelop his land.

Poised at a moment of destiny and facing the cyclonic whirl of changes that threaten to shake its very foundations, Kusumpur symbolises the ever-relevant theme of confrontation between tradition and modernity. This conflict becomes more pronounced if the tradition is as hoary and ancient as the self of a nation that is India. Man in his hesitance is an amalgam of history carrying the whole tradition of earth in his blood, and must confront the new and the unknown in his forward march. Neither the individual nor a nation can avoid this unalterable fact of the human predicament. It is in such a handling of a wide, yet precise and well-defined theme where the universal and the particular coalesce and merge that Manoj Das reveals an ancient ancestral insight. "History is a symbol," says Sri Krishnaprem, "and what that symbol signifies is something infinitely more precious than a mere peddling adherence to a sequence of so-called 'facts'" (Roy, *Yogi* 134).

With its cooing cuckoos and blooming Krishnachura trees, the "fairytale world" of Kusumpur is verily a primordial Eden of innocence, harmony and beauty. But the fall from Eden is not far: "The whole village looked bewildered the day the Krishnachura trees were felled" (1-2). This is the first whiff of change, brought about by Englishmen in furtherance of their war-time preparations of building an airstrip and a dam. The attending devastation of nature that comes with 'development' is meaningfully suggested. The degradation of man is soon to follow: Rajni, the village vagabond, "who had served in the city for many years" is the first to explore the Englishmen's colony and comes home drunk. "Never before had Kusumpur seen a drunken man" (3); nor had it possibly been a witness to the felling of Krishnachura trees! At this turn of events, the villagers with their limited knowledge and simple psychology are certainly disoriented if not panicky:

> The village elders met time and again—and every time they sat late into the night—in an effort to resolve the mystery of the alien activities along the verge of their valley. They knew of the great war that was being fought in the land of the Sahibs, above the clouds and deep in the sea. They suspected that the hustle at their doorstep had something to do with it.... Inscrutable was the way of the Sahibs, they concluded, and decided to wait and see (2).

When Rajni dies next morning from an overdose of drinking, the villagers' faith in a providential order is vindicated. "Many found in the incident a mystic endorsement of the belief that all was not lost with the laws of Dharma, that one could not just launch a horrendous whim and hope to get away with it" (5).

If that was a whiff of change, now comes the gale: the village had just been hit by fury of an unprecedented cyclone when arrives a party of relief workers from "the land where women dress like men." It "was the first time the people of Kusumpur had seen a young woman in trousers" (35). Reena's disbelief at finding that the villagers lived without a newspaper and had never heard of a radio-set reveals in a telling manner the incongruity of the two island worlds. The technological backwardness of the village, however, cannot rob it of its pristine purity and innocence; when Reena is surprised to see a couple of parrots landing close to her and exclaims, "Are they domesticated?" Sudhir's reply is simple—"They live in the nearby forest and they have not learnt to fear the villagers" (37). The threat to the villagers is not posed by this lady with her goggles, binoculars and camera; it comes from two of her male companions; Kamal and Shyam. Kamal, Reena's brother and heir to an industrial house, is a sly, opportunist businessman who works slowly from behind to exploit a situation or relationship. Taking advantage of an idealistic strain in Sudhir's nature by promising to build a cultural institution in Kusumpur, he acquires a fifty-acre plot from him to lease it out later "at a very high price to a party that intends setting up a factory to whip out bottles of shame—I mean liquor" (120). Kusumpur surely has not forgotten Rajni and his bottle!

Less sinister than Kamal's, though more vociferous, confrontational and warped, is the challenge that comes from Shyam, a missionary in the ranks of leftist ideology. The ridiculousness of this aberration of history becomes obvious in comrade Shyam's maiden speech at Kusumpur:

> It was now Shyam's turn. He stood up, swept his defiant hair back from his forehead and began, his voice ringing. The audience looked frightened.... But the situation took an unexpected turn. A lunatic who roamed the region—some took him to be a mystic mendicant and some a jolly vagabond—suddenly appeared behind Shyam. First he made faces. Then, delighted and inspired by the speaker's histrionics, he began to dance. While Shyam raised his voice, scale by scale, to its highest in an effort to wake the dormant conscience of his listeners and to transform them into rebels, the audience looked more and more amused (42).

The meeting ends with the audience shouting *Hari bol*—Glory to God—and Shyam ruefully comments, "We distributed alms, and they sang God's glory." When the relief-party returns home, Shyam stays on in Kusumpur to build a mass-base for his movement. The villagers fail to understand why he is "mingling with some of the most undesirable elements in the neighbourhood." All that Brindavan can say is, "The world, no doubt, is changing fast" (45). When the news that the Kheya is to be closed falls like a thunderbolt on the village, Shyam laps the situation to stir and organise the villagers in a formidable work force. His callous hypocrisy is ironically exposed when he says:

> Whether the river is wiped off or not is of secondary importance. What we must understand is that here is an opportunity to make the people act collectively, something they have never done, to rouse them to their right to agitate, to give them a taste of the thrill of resistance (63).

Such a framework of thought is totally alien to the simple people of Kusumpur. Their feelings find utterance in Sudhir's voice: "we just cannot see our Kheya done to death. It would be barbaric. I'd rather die myself" (62). Shyam's ill-fated revolutionary passion takes its toll in his own languishing and unattended death, and in Rathi's unhealthy conversion that leads to his victimisation and police torture. Rathi, who could not even hurt a simple monkey, becomes militant under Shyam's tutelage and acquires an image of a dangerously violent character (98-99). What detrimental effects can an alien and undigested thought-system have on a simple and trusting psyche of Indian youth is effectively told in the story of these two.

The influences that seep one after another into Kusumpur's placid life seem to come from an outside world which is wide, dark, sinister and malevolent. Their sequence too has an eerie ring of a rising crescendo. The Hindus of Kusumpur and the Muslims on the other side in the *bastee* have always lived in amity. The communal frenzy, "this mad explosion of stupid fear" as Sudhir calls it (126), is a new unknown element that descends upon the innocent lives of Kusumpur. It is an ugly price they pay for their widening horizons in the wake of Freedom and Partition. The politicians and communal leaders have unwittingly become agents of evil. It comes as a revelation that weapons supplied to Hindus and Muslims by their respective protectors have originated from the same factory. The Evil, like God, is one and cannot be the monopoly of any one religion. When Ravi mentions that people have become courageous after possessing these newly-found weapons, Sudhir's thoughtful comment makes the reader reconsider many of his unquestioned premises: "Are you sure you fellows are not possessed by these things?" (126). Further on, Sudhir stands observing the movements of a communal mob:

> Many in the procession swung clubs and some brandished swords. None of them looked like a goonda. Some even looked respectable.... But now their eyes gave out spooky sparks and their limbs throbbed under the impact of something weird that possessed them, something they could not control even if they had wanted to.
>
> Sudhir even saw in a flash, or he thought that he saw, swarms of wasps circling round the heads of the processionists stinging poison into them. It was an eerie

sensation, for Sudhir knew that even though he saw them they were not physical (144-45).

Manoj Das's treatment of the communal cyclone is spread over nearly a quarter of the book and is one of the very best expositions of this seemingly insoluble and ever-present malady of Indian psyche. Not only the simple villagers of Kusumpur and Haru Mia from the other side, ordinary prostitutes like Lalita and common men and women in the city, but also a retired Under-Secretary to the Government, a direct disciple of Soumyadev, and Sudhir himself who has the benign and living presence of Soumyadev to fall back upon, have all fallen prey to this diabolical dance of human insanity. In the closing chapters where Sudhir roams the riot-torn theatre of violence in the city, he remains in a semi-conscious daze of a man whose psyche has been effectually paralysed. The novel successfully portrays the multifarious contours of this cancer but steers clear from providing a solution, for there is none, except dropping a few hints and suggestions here and there: "Let me tell you what I believe: true unity can be realised only by our rising above arguments, above the past and, if you will bear with me, above religions too" (155).

The ravaging invasions of Kusumpur's idyllic innocence cannot be completed without that most deadly of viruses, the hypocritical self-seeking politician of contemporary India, giving it the final blow. Seth Mukund Das and his son and brothers have branched out in different but invariably safe directions, avoiding a direct and demanding involvement in the freedom-struggle, to amass opportunities for expanding their family wealth, influence and power. It is Seth Mukund Das who rescues Sudhir from jail and transforms him from an ordinary riot-prisoner into a glorified freedom-fighter. Ironically, it is the Seth again who announces to a bewildered Sudhir the shape of things to come. He really has the gift of the gab:

> Kusumpur's metamorphosis is no less miraculous than a worm changing into a beautiful butterfly. It is marked out to be the headquarters of a new sub-division. I assure you it will grow into a busy little town in no time. And, Sudhirji, who do you think should be the leader, the spokesman, the guardian, the symbol of the new-born place?

Sudhir, on the other hand, would be glad to escape from Seth's tentacles: "Sethji, please allow me to get off here" (161).

As we reach the last pages, we actually find Kusumpur slowly changing into a market town. Though a circus acrobat in the village fair is still called 'Hanuman,' a new element of militancy, of violence, has found its way into the village atmosphere: "We refuse to be bamboozled! We refuse to be hoodwinked! ...Drag the chap out. We'll teach him how to jump!" (180). Until now, this kind of language was unheard of in Kusumpur.[2]

It is another dimension, quite other than this twice too solid and sullied waking reality, that intervenes through Sudhir and saves Kusumpur and its people from an impending catastrophe. Is it compassion or is it pity? Sudhir muses:

> But, suspended above the throng he realised that his decision was independent of all that. Or, maybe, he had just transcended these considerations at the instance of his new-found friendship with the breeze, the clouds that appeared excited at his approaching their domain, and the couple of stars that peeped through a momentary crack in the clouds but managed to whisper a world of things. Stars had never been so meaningful to him, though whatever they whispered was beyond meaning.

The author seems to suggest that our salvation from a chaos that is ever closing upon us inch by inch lies in our discovering just that other dimension of living. He reasserts Rousseau and Wordsworth but in a way that is rooted in his own soil. Here good and evil seek a reconciliation and transcendence, not an eternal Semitic confrontation and conflict. If Kusumpur stands for Earth as the eternal soil of flowering, a recurring birth of Divine in Matter, Lalita, the fallen woman, bears the title name of the Divine Mother from *Srilalitasahasranamastotram,* the thousand names of the Divine Mother.

IV

But what kind of place is Kusumpur? The answer involves an exploration into the strangeness, wonder and mystery of a land called India. With its sea, river and forest, birds, flowers and evening sounds, and a river being done to death, Kusumpur is a typical Oriya village where Manoj Das himself was born and grew up.[3] But as the physical features blur and one enters the dark, mysterious and deeper life of Kusumpur, one stands facing a typical Indian world of rustic idiom, humour, and superstitions and legends that border on occult. An occurrence of death in this village, whether of one or many, brings out such a rich texture of suffering and compassion that it almost completes the Indian vision of life.

In days before the action opens in the novel, Kusumpur, the valley of flowers, used to be a "fairytale world" where spring was naturally announced by the coos of cuckoos. In tune with the rhythm of life "the boys raised a sporadic riot of songs; the girls hummed, smiling at one another." From the Chowdhury villa, the house of the village zamindar, emanated notes *of Rag Vasant,* and "the cluster of Krishnachura trees that marked the frontier burst into blood-red flowers" (1). But now the trees have been felled and the village has decayed. Both Hari Chowdhury and Roy Sahib, the neighbouring zamindars, have taken to opium and are losing their way into a world of phantoms and unreality. The old is either dead or dying, the new as yet in a cauldron awaiting a definite formation. Manoj Das achieves a rare fusion of subjective and external in his narrative and we find man and Nature, individual and the cosmic, merging into a single landscape: "The sun had set and the western sky looked weird with an unusually large splash of vermilion across it. The twilight, as usual, cast a shade of melancholy on the discoloured and desolate house" (4). Soon we come to know that the Chowdhuries for generations have suffered from melancholy, the millennial tames of the Indian nation.

Kusumpur's natural surroundings—containing a tinge of supernatural as well—have cast a spell on Sudhir and made him one of its own. His own parents being nowhere visible on the scene, it is Nature who, more than anyone else, has been responsible for Sudhir's nurture. Desolate and lonely, a child no older than five, Sudhir receives the blessed gift of his first initiation into the mystery of Nature. We have here such an evocative portrayal of man's communion with Nature that it needs to be quoted at some length:

> One night, after the old woman had fallen asleep, Sudhir crept out of the house alone and toddled up the narrow road leading to the river bank. Cicadas buzzing in the grass on both sides of the road fell silent as he passed by. Their gesture reassured him of his own existence, however small.
>
> Once on the river-bank he burst into sobs. Then he gazed at the sky for a long time as though to discover the particular star which had dropped him in this alien world. His moist eyes read a message of consolation in the soothing arrows of light that the stars sent him.
>
> Across the meadows that spread on the other side of the river, drops of light twinkled in unknown and faraway houses. They, too, seemed to respond to his heart-throbs. Even the forest beside the meadow, a castle built of darkness, seemed willing to embrace his tiny body in a show of affection. Then there was the song of the sea, when all else was silent, that spoke to his heart....
>
> He repeated his secret trips to the river-bank night after night. He no longer wept. He was in love with the night and the silence (12-13).

The echoes of *Doctor Zhivago* and Wordsworth can be heard from a distance.

Since then the discovery has ever stayed with him. Back from the college, now a fully grown up man, Sudhir is watching the rain come and feels "he could run for miles along the river-bank spotting the small boats hidden behind the screen of rain" (18). A little later, after having spent an anxious night watching over his ailing beloved from yonder childhood days, Sudhir tiptoes to the roof to regain himself: "A glow had begun to tint the east. A flock of birds flew across the horizon. Sudhir felt a deep affinity with the quiet dawn" (29).

Wordsworth's vision of Nature's education finds its total fulfilment in Sudhir. His spontaneity, compassion, generosity, courage, and above all a simple transparent self are the gifts of Nature he has received by living and trusting in her close proximity. When life forces his steps towards the town and city, we can clearly mark that he is a fish out of water. He tries to mingle with the so-called important and powerful people at the Seth's party, "But they seemed alien and remote to him. Suddenly he felt restless and longed for Kusumpur" (75).

Reena, the Seth's much pampered daughter, is a study in contrast. As she comes in contact and opens to Nature's influences in Kusumpur, we discover that Nature has a rejuvenating power that can heal a wounded psyche. This is her first evening at Kusumpur:

> Twilight was changing into evening. Kamal, Sujan and Shyam sat engrossed in their thoughts. Reena alone was alert to the quiet happenings around—the hidden sunbeams making the clouds on the sea look like citadels of gold—the whole sky gradually changing into a vast and enigmatic smile at the earth—the dusk slowly reducing the trees and the houses to sad clumsy forms—the weird howling of jackals, a solitary star popping out of a milky patch of cloud, and then a flood of stars changing the sky into a domain of light and remoteness, dim lights beginning to twinkle through hedges, jackals proving more vigorous on their second howling, and then, for the first time after the cyclone, the sound of conch-shells and cymbals coming from the temple (38).

For one who is born in a town and has lived and travelled all her life only through din and noise, Kusumpur is an epiphany of marvellous discovery: "I have never known so much silence.... I have never known such luxuriant darkness either. It is magnificent—like a mother!" (38-39). Is she reading into Keats's Nightingale or is this the intent and significance of reading all poetry? Nature, the mother of all beings, has reclaimed one more of her children.

When Reena returns to the town after five days in Kusumpur, she is a changed woman who has dropped her binoculars, goggles, camera and trousers to don that elegant Indian sari. Her letter to Sudhir confirms her own awareness of this deep change:

> My eyes look different—say my friends. Why not? Did I not have them steeped in the blue of your sky—the sky

over Kusumpur? They further say that even my voice has changed. I am not surprised. Did I not spend my four fabulous days listening to words of innocence? (60).

Steeped in the primal innocence and so close to Nature, man lives in possession of other sense organs than merely the physical. He retains a magical visionary power[4] and his perception of Reality is different from a dry rationalist's neatly-arranged lifeless schemata. Call it fantastic, hallucinatory, superstitious, ignorant, or sublime and occult, there is this Indian life-vision, vibrant, many-coloured, dream-like, a weaving as if of Maya, spread all over from cover to cover on the pages of this magnificent work of Manoj Das.

Here in this world people have a strange set of beliefs that function at various socio-psychological levels. Building *a pukka* house is considered dangerously inauspicious: "The head of the family was likely to die before the completion of the work" (22). The daughters of the village are sacred and call for total protection: "They are eyed by a hundred evil beings as soon as they are out of our house" (30). Conversely, Rathi's childlike acceptance of the village priest's authority that a spy would be born in a future incarnation "as a beast, to be lured and entrapped treacherously by a hunter!" can lead to corrective behaviour "through confession, repentance, and sacrifice" (91). Durgawati, suffering from a deadly leprosy, is quite convinced that "I'm atoning for my sins of a previous life or for the sins of others" (10). This kind of calm philosophical resignation, so ingrained in the Indian psyche, helps Ravi to bear all that 'Life brings with her in her equipage:' "The experience must have been necessary for us, whatever be the incidents that caused them. We suffered the cyclone. Did we question the cyclone's right to cause us suffering?" (99).

But this is not all. Believe it or not, the village has a real Ghosts' Corner full of imps and vampires. Then there is the legend of Chowdhury tiger: the 'great-great-great-great grandfather' of Sudhir Chowdhury who, by reciting a secret mantra, could change himself into a tiger (49-50). A little away from Kusumpur, there is a pond where two lovers were treacherously done to death and "till my grandfather's time, if travellers camped under the banyan trees here on rainy nights, the wind carried to them the lovers' faint dialogues from the lake" (95).

Perhaps the whole of life is a metaphor and there is no such thing as exclusively physical. The villagers are not only adept in the art of reading the signs (55), they can also perhaps descry the strange invisible spirit of the cyclone:

> It was rumoured that something uncanny had taken place during the last phase of the cyclone. Luminous as a meteor, a being sped through space riding a flying horse, crying out, "Calm! Calm!" Only then did the cyclone begin to subside. The consensus was that the daring goddess was the spirit of cyclones in the process of withdrawing her fury....
>
> However, it was not easy to come across eye-witnesses. The only two persons at Kusumpur who were believed to have seen the goddess and heard her command were Raghu Naik and Nishamoni. No wonder one should die and the other grow dumb (25).

It is the author's characteristic style that in the face of supernatural or irrational he maintains a conspicuously ambivalent stance or sounds a trifle ironical at the most.

No reading of Kusumpur's life can ever be complete without taking into account its response to death, the most central and meaningful of all episodes in life where natural and supernatural come together in an intimate embrace. Here, we have first a general and widespread occurrence of havoc and death caused by the cyclone, then the death of the individuals—Brindavan, Navin Contractor, Shyam and Vishnupriya. But one death that stands out by its sheer force of poignancy, significance and details is that of Brindavan.

Brindavan's death is the passing away of an age, an order, a way of life. It comes so suddenly, is so unnecessary and unrelated to the whole, just like a very real death, that it makes the reader cry with the author, "Brindavan's death seemed abrupt to the point of absurdity" (57). No deus ex machina to further a plot, to develop a storyline, in no way helpful to anything at all, it is just there, so needless and yet a brazen matter of fact round the corner!

Unknown to himself that he is Brindavan's illegitimate son, as Sudhir pours *Gangajal,* the sacred water of the Ganges, little by little, into the dying man's mouth, we read an added meaning in Brindavan's words: "Babu, you are kind as a god. Your visit has changed my destiny." Sudhir's perception of death is symbolic and at the same time so close to the actuality of the process:

> He was reminded of the lanterns on the small boats sailing on the Kheya as he sat watching them at night. He was overwhelmed by the same vague sadness he used to feel looking at the phantom figures beside those lanterns being reduced to smudges and then dissolving in the mist as the boats receded (54).

Rendered in a masterly evocative prose, this is a rare insight into the phenomenon of death.

In spite of having once indulged in an amorous misadventure—perchance his name has something to do with it—Brindavan has lived a life of piety, devotion and straightforwardness. As he struggles to speak his last few words to his wife, possibly to make a confession of his long-held secret, it is the lady who, like a true Indian wife, has the last word: "I know all you wish to say. Remain calm. Think only of the lotus feet of the Lord" (55). At the end of life, spiritual well-being is the only thing that matters. And Brindavan receives it in plenty.

When the priest, chanting *Hari bol,* enters the house to reveal that his efforts at the temple to win life for Brindavan have failed, we see in him formulated a whole village's concern for Brindavan and get ready to accept the inevitability of death. Soon after, the two Vaishnava monks with their *mridungum* arrive at Brindavan's bedside and, chanting Lord's glory, give a fitting requiem to the departing soul. Just coincidence, or part of a wider scheme of things, it restores our faith in an immemorial order of a foreseen design. It is an extraordinarily well-written piece and the whole of chapter 12 must be read in full to get a feel of its total impact.

V

If in Kusumpur, nestling among trees and rivers, the evening begins with a regular *puja* at the Kalika temple, a public function ends with the shouts of *Hari bol,* and the ubiquitous Sadhu baba and wandering mendicants are part of everyday life, it is quite logical that on moving deeper into the heart of Nature's sanctuary, a dense and more primal forest, we should discover the mystic dynamo that lies at the heart of Kusumpur's environing vibrations. As one moves with Sudhir who is led as if by a quirk of fate to seek refuge from the irrational twists and turns of the human world at the feet of Soumyadev, one stands face to face with an authentic experience at the centre of Indian life. Having learnt the art of communing with Nature and been gifted by her Grace with spontaneity, love, compassion and courage, Sudhir is truly a romantic ready to graduate to mysticism.

The three chapters—19 to 21—describing Sudhir's sojourn at Soumyadev's hermitage give us a meticulously well-crafted exposition of Indian mystical tradition. Sadhu Sadanand leads Sudhir and his companions to "one of the last great forests with a mythical past" where the hermitage is situated. As they enter the forest, their talk touches another plane of reality. Someone asks a question about snakes, and the Sadhu's reply is rather uncanny: "Let us not utter the creature's name—it is very sensitive—but it never strikes for fun" (100). More than a mere superstition, it sounds like an occult experienced truth. Sudhir is surprised as he watches a subtle change taking place in his mental state: suddenly, everything is credible and anything could be real and possible. One remembers Nachiketas in the Kathopanishad where in the very second verse, before any action could commence, we read: "As the gifts were led past, faith took possession of him who was yet a boy unwed and he pondered." What happens to Sudhir is neither fiction nor fancy. Ask anyone frequenting authentic ashrams in this country, and they will aver that it is a very common experience.

As Sudhir moves further into the forest towards the hermitage, his perception, touching on psycho-mystical, gets deeper. Flashes of insight leap into that awakened state of awareness: "To live was like wading through such darkness, with no more light than a lantern could provide." Doubts raise their head only to dissolve into clarity. Everything comes alive and distinctions between animate and inanimate blur.

Sadhu Sadanand chants his morning mantras and, "For a moment it appeared to Sudhir that the Sadhu's audience was not limited to their small party; the trees slowly recovering their forms, the birds and beasts in the process of waking up, and even the stars fading out, heard him" (102). Sudhir's first meeting with Soumyadev where not a word is spoken is equally revealing[5]:

> Sudhir hesitated and then bowed down. When he raised his head Soumyadev's smile had grown brighter. Sudhir felt as if his inner being was bathed in a cool shower of jasmine flowers! The experience was unexpected.
>
> A sweet weight of gratitude pulled him down. He fell at the hermit's feet before he knew what he was doing (103).

He is introduced to Vikashananda who comes from an affluent family, been abroad for higher studies and holds a Master's degree in philosophy. On their first meeting, Vikashananda's well-argued remarks demolish Sudhir's mental framework and reduce man's pompous achievements to bare nothingness:

> I have seen enough of your wide world and your humanity, have frequently mingled with your elite and have felt amazed at the poverty of their concepts, have explored your poetry and philosophy and have been scandalised at their hollowness, have stood amidst magnificent ruins of civilisations and have observed the doings of men and their undoing by time. Who could have imagined that I should at last land in this obscure jungle and find the stuff for which my soul thirsted? (104).

Sudhir is slowly settling down to discover a new way of life when Reena, on being informed by Ravi, appears at the hermitage to take Sudhir to the town. Having discovered the fragrance of Nature at Kusumpur, and disenchanted with the loveless surroundings of her home, Reena has grown into a nice beautiful soul like Shakespeare's Miranda who figures in one of Soumyadev's discussions. She cares for every form of life and is always ready to be of help to anyone who needs her. Her encounter with Soumyadev is that of a sceptic meeting an authentic embodiment of Indian spiritual tradition. Her questions—Have you seen God? Can you show me some miracle?—are simple but the most frequently asked ones.

Soumyadev's dialogues with Reena are not meant to bring out his depth or greatness. They just suggest how a beginner on the path is to begin by questioning his presumptions. They are hints for a possible initiate, veiled mantras that could change the hearer's life if he cared to listen.

Sudhir's continued stay at the ashram leads him to a widening silence and consequently a thinning of his ego-self. He shows neither interest nor curiosity in Soumyadev's miraculous powers. He is content to love the man and be loved by him in turn. He has learnt to look upon life "as a perpetual process of growth, a journey from the prison-house of one's ego into infinity's freedom" (114). But he is not asked to renounce the world and lead a monastic life. When the moment of choice arrives, he is told by Sadhu Sadanand: "You must follow your *Swadharma*—the inner law of your being" (116). The chapters devoted to Sudhir's stay in the ashram are not meant to be a treatise on mysticism, but they do provide sufficient hints and answer some very basic questions.

The mystic's multifaceted influence is not limited to the four walls of his hermitage. His silent presence is unobtrusively widespread, bringing solace to a tortured soul, guiding the waylaid and making the crooked straight. His disciples with their different natures come from a variety of backgrounds, and each one represents a particular human knot. Vikashananda with his academic laurels and foreign education can easily add spiritual glamour to a rich man's social parties (137) and with an equal mastery of "the art of seduction" (156) can take that rich man's young and beautiful daughter to America (157). Shobhananda with his '*desi*' background is rather jealous of Vikashananda's adventures and has decided therefore to keep the field of his exploits within the country. He is passionately involved in the communal riots and, with an ideological commitment, intends "blowing up with dynamite the mosque that stands on Krishna's birthplace at Mathura" (154). His repentance, however, at Vikashananda's downfall gives him a saving grace, and we see how each one of us, both saint and sinner, is progressing in one's own way. Everything finds a reflection here, in one way or another, for which the Indian mystic is admired—knowledge, grace, askesis and experience, and also of which he is accused—fundamentalism, scandal, and an unruly body of followers and disciples.

VI

If the treatment of theme and setting in *Cyclones* reveals a truly Indian way of looking at Reality, no less obvious is the essential Indianness of perception in Manoj Das's portrayal of his characters. Sudhir is the lone major character in the novel, all others being minor but significant portions of a larger group-soul. While Sudhir is clearly an emerging individual face of the collective universal matrix of Indian psyche, the others are faint glimmerings of an as yet withdrawn undifferentiated whole.

Like Hardy's rustics, Manoj Das's minor characters, particularly his villagers, have a peculiar and robust charm of their own. They are simple, innocent, ignorant, philosophical, idiosyncratic, committed to values, given to fun and folly, forbearing and always a wee bit closer to God. There is no inherent evil in them but they do get contaminated sometime by an unknown alien poison like that of a leftist ideology or a sinister communal hatred.

Each one of them has an individuality of his own and is yet so much like his earth which nourishes him. There is Hari Chowdhury, the decadent zamindar given to melancholy, misfortune and opium, who cries innocently like a baby on meeting his estranged wife. Brindavan, his manager, is an honest, devoted and methodical worker who uses craft and guile to get even with Roy, his master's adversary. Keeping it ever a secret in his heart that Sudhir is his illegitimate son, he yet struggles to do all he can to bring back a measure of respectability to Sudhir's position as the scion of the Chowdhuries. He arranges for Sudhir's formal adoption and is keen on getting a wife for him from a noble family. Ravi, Brindavan's grandson and formally adopted son, is a study in the Indian tradition of Hanuman-like selfless service. Roy Sahib, the ruined zamindar of Lalgram, is a character straight from a village opera who carries his ancestral enmity with the Chowdhuries as a sacred burden and bequeaths it in perpetual legacy to his daughter, Geeta, at his death. Duryodhana, the village simpleton will go to any length to atone for his innocent breach of trust. Then there are the village elders, Rajni, Rathi, and the ubiquitous Sadhu baba, all contributing a shade of their own to the colourful life of Kusumpur.

But it is to Sudhir that we must turn to fathom the secrets and essence of Indian persona. The very first thing that strikes us about this man is his illegitimate birth. There is no structural necessity, either antecedent or consequent, that demands such a background. His mother, Usha, is simply mentioned, not shown, and her affair with Brindavan is not at all discussed in the book. The background no doubt hurts Sudhir, but leaves no such scar as to affect his constitutional personality. And yet the whole thing never leaves the reader's mind. Is there a deeper meaning, a hidden authorial intention, behind it? Is this birth in some way symbolic of the human predicament? Man is born from a union of mind and body, of spirit and matter. In a state of affairs where spiritualists deny matter and materialists cry foul of spirit, it is quite understandable that a union of spirit and matter can be nothing but illegitimate. If the name 'Brindavan' can even distantly point towards Krishna, the Divine Soul, the Rig Veda makes amply clear the meaning of Usha: "She follows to the goal of those that are passing on beyond, she is the first in the eternal succession of the dawns that are coming,—Usha widens bringing out that which lives, awakening someone who was dead.... She desires the ancient mornings and fulfils their light (I. 113. 8, 10—Sri Aurobindo's translation).

Another trait which distinguishes Sudhir from most protagonists in either contemporary Indian or Western fiction is the very manner in which he is presented to us. He looks more like a process, a movement, without a beginning or end, rather than a distinctly formed individual. In a total absence of the self-conscious ego—he has to wrestle with the hidden one while residing with Soumyadev—there is no doer in him planning, projecting and seeking after a desired fulfilment. He is a drifter, except that the word carries a pejorative connotation. More truly he can be seen as floating with Tao, carried forward on currents of a vaster Nature. Things always happen to him and he is glad to accept them as they come and go. He has the stance of an impartial witness, a choiceless observer, moving as if mounted on a machine, *yantrarudhen mayaya,* to use an apt expression from the Gita.

He is not a natural son of Hari Chowdhury but is made to inherit the mantle of the Chowdhuries. As a young man he avoids Kusumpur and has no desire to settle in there, and yet when he is forced to come back, he falls in love with the place and becomes a naturalised native. Temperamentally, he is a calm and quiet person, but finds himself in a fit of anger, possessed as if by some external force, threatening to behead Navin Contractor. When the contractor is actually beheaded the next day, Sudhir is certain that his "arrest cannot be prevented" (92). It is Ravi then who arranges for his removal to a safe place; Sudhir simply acquiesces to the plan without any resistance. Thus is he led, as if by destiny, to the feet of Soumyadev. When he resists Reena's pressure and refuses to leave the ashram, it is not his self-will but a will united with Soumyadev's that makes him stand his ground. When Brindavan's wife, Vishnupriya, calls him back from her deathbed to Kusumpur, it is for him the call of his destiny but he accepts it only with his Guru's consent. Even when he acts decisively, once to avert the tragedy of a communal riot in Kusumpur and a second time in the acrobat scene to abort an imminent riot by an unruly mob, it is an unknown impulse that takes over him and he acts merely as an agent and instrument. At the end when the Seth has manipulated an almost assured political future for Sudhir, we leave him undeserving, non-committal and unresisting. The closing sentence of the book reads: "He stretched himself on the grass and waited for the sunrise [is it Usha, his mother?] to lead his steps" (183).

Is he a dreamer or a lover who falls in love even with parrots and prostitutes? Is he a fatalist or simply a junkie—Hari Chowdhury was an opium eater—and a plain spineless creature whom anyone can take for a ride (Kamal does take him twice)? Sudhir is that essential authentic Indian whom the West, due to its total lack of any worthwhile understanding of the East, has dubbed a quietist, defeatist, fatalist and primitive. To the western myopic eye Sudhir cannot appear in any other way; he is just that: there is no use defending him. But the secret of Indian character will not be found in Derrida and I.A. Richards; it must be sought back home in Indian scriptures. Aware of its finite self which has no independent existence separated from its source, the Indian mind, aspiring for a conscious union with the Infinite, awaits its behest in a calm and quiet repose:

Nabhinandeta maranam nabhinandeta jivanam:
Kalameva pratiksheta nirdesham bhrityako yatha.
Death nor life I hymn, but wait
Like time upon His guidance still:
I bow to what He would dictate
As a servant doing his master's will
(*Mahabharata,* Shantiparva, Roy, *Sri Aurobindo* 390).

NOTES AND REFERENCES

1. Further references to *Cyclones* carry only page numbers.
2. We have noted the various forces that bring about a cyclonic upheaval to a rather calm and quiet life in Kusumpur. Not all changes, however, that enter Kusumpur are malevolent. Sudhir's education and his interaction with town-folk have brought a few things that are quite healthy and redeeming in nature. He has found a footing from where he can speak to English Sahibs, politicians and bureaucracy with an air of confidence and a sense of equality. It has freed him from many superstitions and social taboos. Sudhir is also responsible for bringing an allopath, another first in Kusumpur, when Brindavan is fatally ill. He also brings his knowledge of practical sciences to eradicate Geeta's superstitious belief that "water is forbidden in fever" (29).
3. In an article on Orissa Manoj Das wrote: "When I had first visited in 1954, events supernatural were looked upon as most natural and the villagers heard mysterious incantations and the sound of conchshells from the interior of the ancient forest. Less than a decade later the entire forest had disappeared, multi-storeyed buildings blinded the horizon, trees looks stupefied, smeared with thick dust continuously sprayed by roaring trucks. The pretty little branch of the Mahanadi that girdled the village had been choked to death" (quoted in Raja, 60).
4. See, for example, Sudhir's ecstatic vision of Reena as she comes out of the sea all dressed in fire and flames. Ironically, to Sudhir's dry rationalist friends this vision can only be explained as "an optical illusion" (51).
5. Matthieu Ricard, a Frenchman who had just completed his doctoral

thesis under a Nobel laureate in molecular biology, recounts a similar experience of his first meeting with a Buddhist monk. Ricard hardly knew any English and the monk's son who acted as an interpreter had only a stammering knowledge of English: "I sat opposite him [the monk] all day long, and had the impression that I was doing what people call 'meditating,' in other words simply collecting myself in his presence. I received a few words of teaching, almost nothing. His son, Tulku Pema Wangyal, spoke English, but I could hardly understand a word. It was his person, his being, that made such an impression on me; the depth, strength, serenity and love that emanated from him and opened my mind.... In his presence, however, I'd intuitively discovered one of the basic things about the teacher-disciple relationship, putting one's mind in harmony with that of the teacher. It's called 'mixing your mind with the teacher's mind', the teacher's mind being wisdom and our mind being confusion. What happens is that by means of that 'spiritual union' you pass from confusion to wisdom" (Revel 7-8, 9).

WORKS CITED

Anand, Mulk Raj, "Pigeon-Indian: Some Notes on Indian-English Writing." *Aspects of Indian Writing in English*. Ed. M.K. Naik. Delhi: The Macmillan Company of India Limited, 1979, 24-44.

Aurobindo, Sri, *The Foundations of Indian Culture*. Pondicherry: Sri Aurobindo Ashram, 1971.

Cassirer, Ernst, *Language and Myth*. Trans. Susanne Langer. *The Theory of Criticism*. Ed. Raman Seldon. London: Longman Group UK Limited, 1988, 111-113.

Das, Manoj, *Cyclones: A Novel*. New Delhi: Sterling Publishers Private Limited, 1987.

——. *Farewell to a Ghost*. New Delhi: Penguin Books India (P) Ltd., 1994.

Jussawalla, Adil, Ed. *New Writing in India*. Harmondsworth: Penguin Books Ltd., 1974.

Prem, Sri Krishna, and Sri Madhava Ashish, *Man, the Measure of All Things: In the Stanzas of Dzyan*. Adyar, Madras: The Theosophical Publishing House, 1966.

Raja, P., *Many Worlds of Manoj Das*. Delhi: B.R. Publishing Corporation, 1993.

Revel, Jean-Francois and Matthieu Ricard. *The Monk and the Philosopher*. Trans. John Canti. London: Thorsons, Harper Collins, 1999.

Roy, Dilip Kumar, *Sri Aurobindo Came to Me*. 2nd ed. Pondicherry: All India Books, 1984.

——. Yogi Sri Krishnaprem, 2nd Rev. Ed. Bombay: Bharatiya Vidya Bhavan, 1975.

Verma, Mukesh Ranjan, "Indian English Novel since 1980." *Reflections on Indian English Literature.* Ed. M.R. Verma and K.A. Agrawal. New Delhi: Atlantic Publishers and Distributors, 2002, 1-7.

11

R.K. NARAYAN'S *THE GUIDE:* A STUDY IN FEMINIST PERSPECTIVE

AKHILESHWAR THAKUR

R.K. Narayan's novels belong to a unique genre of fictional writing. For one thing, they are neither allegories nor fairy-tale romances. Again, one may also not find a pervasive paradigm of symbols in his novels notwithstanding some such studies by scholars like Prof. G.S. Amur and P.S. Sundaram. His unique kind of writing is typically an Indian way of balancing life and art, where ideas are interwoven in the very texture of the lives and aspirations of the characters. M.M. Mahood's observation, in this context, is very pertinent:

> ...he is not a drifting water-hyacinth, his art is better typified by the lotus whose shining flower is anchored by a firm stem to the fertile ground beneath. And that ground, like all subsoil, is stratified—by which I mean that it is impossible to read and reread Narayan's novels without coming to the realization that, beneath their gentle record of mundane happening they carry both an analogical and allegorical meaning that events recorded, however trivial, have also a political (in the widest sense of the term) and a metaphysical significance (Mahood 5).

It is for this reason that Narayan's novels are called serious comedies where his genuine social concerns are manifested through the form of his works, ordering of his narrative, tone of his writing, tools of irony and humour and above all through the conception and creation of characters.

This paper attempts at revealing one such genuine social and humane concern in Narayan's novel *The Guide* (1958).

Through a gentle and engaging story this novel displays novelist's serious concern for the vulnerability of, and vicissitudes in, the lives of Indian women. Through the poignant course of Rosie's life Narayan charts the silent anger of Indian womanhood at the futility and meaninglessness of female-life. However, Narayan's voice is not that of a belligerent feminist but of a cool, mature and meditative thinker who sees the problem in the complexities of its configuration with a sensibility rooted deeply in the Indian ethos. His care and concern for the wounded womanhood is related to the purely traditional and scriptural wisdom of yore. And this article proposes to reveal that dimension of Narayan's concern which can be said to be his synthesized feminism, a dimension which is amply illustrated in *The Guide* (1958).

The Guide (1958) reveals the boredom, frustrations and fatigue punctuating the life of an Indian wife, not merely a docile housewife like Savitri of *The Dark Room*, but a woman of substance, endowed with beauty, education and sensibility. Narayan in conceiving and creating the character of Rosie—the name of the wife here—perhaps wants to propose that the salvation of an Indian wife does not lie completely in education. Education may not provide her all that she aspires for. Rosie is more than well qualified, an M.A. in Economics, rarely to be found even in the early decades of post-independence India. Savitri wished if she were educated she would not have suffered and she felt that Kamala and Sumati must study up to B.A. But after two decades, for Rosie education brings no change and for her, too, life is nothing but a protracted tale of suffering. Anger, defeatism and anguish are all she has in her stormy life. She is caught in a web where nobody seems to honour her inner feelings, fulfil her fervent desire, smooth her turbulent mind, cajole her womanly pranks and calm her storm-tossed heart.

She is married to a man who is himself highly educated and a thorough academician, but has no acumen to study the human heart. For the first time when we are told about a conversation between Rosie and her husband we easily glimpse a rift between the couple as narrated by Raju. When the wife talks abut her love for dance and her anxiety to see a King Cobra, the husband rebukes her and calls her interests morbid.

Even if Raju is considered a prejudiced man, who envies Marco in sheer infatuation for Rosie, there is every reason to think that Marco almost could not stand the tastes and temperament of his wife. In one of the conversations, he asks Raju:

> You have probably no notion how to deal with women, have you?
>
> He leant over and said, 'If a man has to have peace of mind it is best that he forget the fair sex' (63).

The attitude of Marco as husband seems to be negligent of womanly feelings. The irony of the situation is that Raju succeeds in pulling Rosie out of the hotel room where a married man has failed to convince his wife. The husband knows not what a great possession a good wife is and he remains in a perpetual illusion about the antagonism between a man and a woman. Narayan ironically points out that Marco has his own shortcomings and blemishes shielding his heart which prevents him from entering into a real fulfilling marital life. Very foolishly Marco calls Raju, 'a wizard' (65) and not knowing, fully, the consequences of it, carelessly observes "You know I have only one principle in life. I don't want to be bothered with small things" (66). Perhaps by small things he means care and concern for a person whom he has married. We are told that on the Mempi Hills "the girl was in ecstasy. She ran like a child from plant to plant with cries of joy, while the man looked on with no emotion. Anything that interested her seemed to irritate him" (67).

Rosie, it seems, wants to live like a complete Indian housewife under the loving tutelage of a caring husband. At the time of dinner she says, "No, no let me serve you both, and I will be the last to eat, like a good housewife" (68). But Marco instead of getting touched by it, receives it coldly and in a rather cavalier vein. Raju's observations that "dead and decaying things seemed to unloosen his tongue and fire his imagination rather that things that lived and moved and swung the limbs" (72), are more than true.

Thus it seems that Marco perhaps married out of a desire to have someone to care for his routine life and Rosie, who herself was a dreamer, wanted a man who could care for her career. This is how Raju sums up the characters of Marco and Rosie. However, notwithstanding Raju's prejudices this summing up of Raju has much substance in it. The incidents and situations betray similar impressions of their married life. Raju, who is himself a reckless picaro, fully exploits the situation and further complicates their lives. Instead of serving as a guide for betterment, he cunningly serves as a foil to Rosie in her predicament. Raju whom Marco had once called a wizard, really acts as one and allures Rosie into his fold. She is blinded and in a moment of utter frustration, willy-nilly, enters into a physical liaison with Raju.

Raju is clearly an opportunist who is not serious about this relationship. His mind is singularly set on exploiting the situation and fulfilling his carnal desire. His careless attitude towards Rosie is more than evident when he talks to the shop-boy who is asking his permission to act as the guide of some tourists. Raju thinks to himself "next, probably, he would ask permission to keep the girl company" (103). For Raju, the company of Rosie is merely an opportunity, least bothering that she happens to be some one else' s wife which he would not allow others to share. He is clearly a man who has lost the balance of his mind and is now blinded by mere infatuation.

But, for Rosie this sort of reluctant relationship is nothing but self-brought agony. In her weakest moment she had allowed Raju to enter her life by obeying the command of her body, but her conscience had never accepted it. Her heart felt strange stirrings and her whole being got tormented by the feelings of guilt and fear. Raju himself, very graphically, recapitulates those moments of her agony:

> In other ways, too, I found it difficult to understand the girl. I found as I went on that she was gradually losing the free and easy manner of her former days. She allowed me to make love to her, of course, but she was also beginning to show excessive consideration for her husband on the hill. In the midst of my caresses she would suddenly free herself and say, 'Tell Gafur to bring the car. I want to go and see him'.... She would shake her head and say, 'After all, he is my husband. I have to respect him. I cannot leave him there' (105).

Rosie's inside is torn to pieces. She is heart-broken and her soul is seared. Yet her conscience does not reconcile to her infidelity. Her grief-stricken self realizes:

> After all.... After all.... Is this right what I am doing? After all, he has been so good to me, given me comfort and freedom, what husband in the world would let his wife go and live in a hotel room by herself, a hundred miles away? (106).

Narayan, thus, makes us feel that Rosie, too, like Savitri, does not vouch for an independent, free and liberalized view of marriage. Marriage for her, too, is sacrosanct. She holds that a wife ought to perform her duties as tradition demands:

> ...as a good man, he may not mind, but is it not a wife's duty to guard and help her husband whatever the way in which he deals with her? (106).

But Rosie never believes that a woman can work her passion alone by herself. She wanted her art to bloom; to show into the limelight; to become famous and well-known; to show to the world her worth, her image and her identity. However, she believed that those could see the light of day only when there was a real companion—a man, a guide and a mentor. And Rosie is here not much unlike Savitri of *The Dark Room* (1938) when she beseechingly asks Raju for help. She seems to be the most hapless creature in the world when she asks Raju in a meek voice:

> Are you also like him?
> Do you also hate to see me dance?

There is enough ground to believe that Rosie has an urge from within which she wants to see growing but not outside the marital relationship. She fancied a husband who could appreciate her passion, honour her desire, admire her art and love to see her soaring in the sky. But unfortunately Marco was far from it. Instead, he proved a typical husband, a complete egotist having more than usual chauvinism. His callous indifference towards Rosie's talent and ruthless crushing of her innocent desire can be measured in every encounter between them.

Marco is not merely a chauvinist, a male egotist who wants to rule over his wife's desire and aspirations but also complacent human being having an insular mind where any idea from outside, let alone that from his wife, is prevented from entering. He seems to be more than a hypocrite, who had been desirous of an educated wife with a university degree but in reality could not stand and appreciate her art and sensibility. He wants a meek, submissive, docile and subservient wife who would act like a nodding machine. However, the reason behind the rift in the relationship and eventually the collapse of the marriage, was not the stubborn nature or obsessive desire of Rosie for dance but her supposed infidelity—the relationship with Raju. Marco could reveal his mind in the end. With anger, contempt and detestation in his eyes, he bursts out:

> You are here because I am not a ruffian. But you are not my wife. You are a woman who will go to bed with anyone that flatters your antics. That's all (134).

Rosie's life with Raju, too, is stormy and turbulent. After her desertion she seeks shelter in Raju's house. Though Raju wants to see her happy and comfortable, she is not warmly received by his mother. She, along with her brother, tries all means, fair and foul, to oust Rosie. Whereas Raju's mother does it with humility and kindness, the belligerent uncle becomes abusive and indecent. They try to bully her to leave the place.

An unknown force and a strange conviction prevent her from departing from there. Hapless and helpless that she is, she remains a mute spectator of the vicissitudes that life exposes her to. In Raju's stubborn attitude towards her safety, she sees a ray of hope and her innocent mind is never able to foresee the sinister design and mercenary calculations soaring in Raju's mind. For him she was 'a gold mine,' and he always dreamt of "a plan to utilize Rosie's services and make money" (144).

Raju's obsession with helping Rosie was fraught with his carnal desires and mammon-worship. Raju was kind to her because he saw a treasure in Rosie. With all her limitations Rosie proves herself a perfect devotee of art. Raju himself recalls that she was a devoted artist; her passion for physical love was falling into pieces and had ceased to be a primary obsession with her. Indeed, she has no physical love for Raju.

In him she sees a mentor, a guide, a connoisseur. But Raju is not what she thinks him to be. He had keenness for the physical charms of Rosie and watching her practise was no love for the 'Bharat Natyam,' but desire for the curves of her body. Raju wanted her body and Rosie had to sacrifice it nonchalantly because she had been helpless and in him she saw love for art and, hence, her dream coming true.

Raju gave her a new name and she entered a new phase of life. The name buried all woes and sufferings of her earlier life. Her name became a public property and her fame soared. In a very short time she became a star and started enjoying the status and halo of a celebrity. Overwhelmed by such a big name and such a wide fame, she expressed her gratitude to Raju. In a sudden gush of passion she would say, "even if I have seven rebirths I won't be able to repay debt to you" (164).

But very soon Rosie is fatigued by the artificialities of life. For her this stage-life becomes boring and she abhors to make-up. Suffocated by the glamour and glitters of this way of life, she desperately wants to tear away the mask. Though she has changed her name, she cannot change her taste and even the new woman in Nalini could relish only flowers and garlands and not the cheques. A big household, a big car and a big circle could amuse Raju, for Rosie they were almost insignificant. While Raju enjoys radiant existence of a social elite, Rosie wonders—"spending two thousand a month on just two of us. Is there no way of living more simply?" (174).

Because Rosie loved dance as an art and for her it was devotion and not profession, she knew no other way of living but with simplicity. She ever remained the same Rosie with elemental virtues of woman—pure, intrinsic and spontaneous. And when she sees Marco's photograph on the middle page of the Illustrated Weekly of Bombay along with a review of his book described as an epoch-making discovery in Indian cultural history, she gets elated, her mind is excited, her heart throbs and she longs to glimpse that book. In utter excitement she reveals the feelings of her heart before Raju. For a moment she forgets the unkind and cruel treatment she had got from him and curses herself for her infidelity. She views her desertion with utmost self-effacement. When Raju tries to remind her the way Marco had left her, she calmly replies:

> I do, and I deserved nothing less. Any other husband would have throttled me then and there. He tolerated my company for nearly a month, even after knowing what I had done (179).

Raju is never able to understand the real Rosie. He is bewildered to find that she has everything at her disposal—name, money and fame—and yet she is ever dissatisfied. She wanted to dance and she got everything dance could bring her; her career had been at its heights and yet she ever remained troubled. Whereas Raju loves the halo around him, Rosie longs for harmony in life. Right from the beginning she aspired for both liberty and love. Earlier she had been fed up with Marco's monotony and now she is exhausted by Raju's rigours. Rosie cynically expresses the meaning of her present life which is punctuated by boredom, frustration, fatigue and aimlessness. She asks Raju with resignation, contempt and cynicism:

> Do you know the bulls yoked to an oil-crusher? They keep going round and round, in a circle, without a beginning or an end? (180).

She is torn inside; she has reached such a pass that life seems to be strange to her. Neither her husband nor is Raju able to understand what Rosie actually thought of life, love and art. While Marco's chauvinistic mind considered Rosie's love for dance disgraceful and ignoble and therefore shied away from it, Raju's mercantile mind in an opportunistic vein makes, capital out of it and, therefore, always clings to it. And in this manner her instinct and fortune are sandwiched between two types of men, both extremists in their own ways.

Raju's skill as an entrepreneur pays him rich dividends and she enjoys a period of immense success, and the money, drink, parties, reputation and acclaim that go with it. As one would expect there is a kind of logic in the reversal—it collapses as suddenly as it comes about. Out of some muddled system of desires, a mixture of anxiety, envy, goodwill carelessness and over-possessiveness, Raju forges Rosie's signature on a document sent to her by the lawyer of Marco. He is sentenced to two year' imprisonment and the radiant phase of his life is summarily terminated. So, the nemesis follows after a brief glow. Raju, like a puerile, doesn't understand the course of human affairs. Rosie, on the other hand, gets bewildered and stunned as she tries to comprehend the situation. With stoic silence inside her, she merely says:

> I felt all along you were not doing right things. This is Karma. What can we do?" (193).

Thus Rosie's life by now reaches a pass similar to that where she had once found herself having been turned out by Marco. Raju seems to her now equally chauvinistic, equally exploitative and equally antagonistic. She could not face the public, could not dance and could not think of living with equal zest and vigour. She sees the complete breakdown of even the mechanical life that she had been leading.

However, Rosie still views Marco with respect and adoration. She has never been venomous or vindictive against Marco. She accuses herself and curses her own infidelity—though she had been driven out by Marco. Rosie had achieved nothing in pursuit of her dance. She had lost yet another battle.

Thus, Rosie did not live the life she had visualised and hence she longs for freedom. Her mind is in a frenzy, she contemplates the meaning and significance of her existence. What she aspired for and what she achieved from it. Has she got anything in herself to offer to the world? Is there anything in the name of her identity? Does she essentially need a man to sustain the vicissitudes of life? Countless questions of this nature come to her mind. She has not been able to find suitable answers to all. She has always remained in a fix, in a perpetual dilemma about the fate of a woman—should she live alone all by herself or share her life with somebody? It is more than clear that she has no faith in the former proposition; she believes in a relationship with a true, just, caring, affectionate man in the name of husband. And marriage remained a sacred institution for her, though hers was a failure. She has seen that there is no alternative to marriage and one must live through it considering it sacrosanct. Marco, Rosie and Raju—all of them have defied it and, therefore, all of them face the wrath of Nature; they are all tormented; and Rosie, being a woman, suffers most.

But Narayan never underestimated the strength of a woman. Instead he sees immense potential in her as an incarnation of 'shakti.' It is very clear when we see Raju realizing his growing jealousy of Rosie's self-reliance and strength in the hours of crisis. Narayan, with subtle irony, points out that Raju gets afraid, instead of becoming happy, to see Rosie going out of his citadel. The novelist puts forth a primeval truth, when he makes Raju confide to himself, about the vitality and prowess of a woman. Men like Marco and Raju should realize their folly in trying things their own ways:

> I knew, looking at the way she was going about her business that she would manage—whether I was inside the bars or outside; whether her husband approved of it or not. Neither Marco nor I had any place in her life, which had its own sustaining vitality and which she herself had underestimated all along (199).

WORKS CITED

Narayan, R.K., *The Guide,* Mysore: Indian Thought Publications, 1958.

Mahood, M., in McLeod, A.L. Ed. *R.K. Narayan: Critical Perspectives,* New Delhi: Sterling Publications, 1994.

12

A POSTMODERN READING OF ARUNDHATI ROY'S *THE GOD OF SMALL THINGS*

YOGESH KUMAR SINHA

The God of Small Things, the first and the only novel written as yet by Arundhati Roy, has been able to create a tremendous academic euphoria, which has not yet subsided even after four years of its publication. Launched on a sea of hype, this literary event of the year 1997, not only initially drew a curiously paradoxical response from Indian audience, reviewers and critics but has also helped generate an industry of critical anthologies as well in the past few years. My paper, as the title suggests, seeks to attempt a postmodern reading of the novel, *The God of Small Things.* However, before attempting to read the novel as a postmodern text, it would be in the fitness of things to at least have an idea of what this elusive term 'postmodernism' is all about. The first part of my paper deals with tracing, in brief, the genealogy of the term 'postmodernism' and its various features and the next part is the analysis of those features in the novel.

I

The term 'postmodernism,' as we know, surfaced in the Anglo-American critical discourse during the 1950s and in a very significant way in the 1960s. Even though critics like Jean Francois Lyotard, Linda Hutcheon, David Lodge etc. have tried to define 'postmodernism,' the term eludes definition so much so that "one critic's postmodernism is another critic's modernism or variant thereof" (Huyssen, 1988, 58-59). Ihab Hassan goes to the extent of saying that "postmodernism suffers from a semantic instability. That is, no clear consensus about its meaning exists among scholars" (Hassan, 1985, 121). David Harvey, however, quotes Jean Francois Lyotard's definition of the postmodern as "incredulity towards metanarratives" (Harvey, 1989, 45).

If modernism means breaking with tradition while still retaining an individualist stance, then postmodernism may well be looked at as interrogating both tradition and individualism. Jeremy Hawthorn refers to Lyotard's treatment of the term 'postmodernism' (Hawthorn, 1998, 142) which refers to:

(a) The non realist and non traditional literature and art of the post Second World War period;

(b) Literature and art which takes certain modernist characteristics to an extreme stage in the form of

  (i) rejection of representation in favour of self-reference,

  (ii) rejection of the sense of the work of art as an organic whole,

  (iii) teasing of the reader for collaboration with him/her,

  (iv) rejection of 'character' and 'plot',

  (v) rejection of meaning itself as a hopeless delusion and;

(c) Aspects of a more general human condition in the late capitalist world of the post 1950s.

Postmodernism, according to Harvey, is mimetic of certain practices—social, economic, political etc.—in the societies in which it appears (Hawthorn, 1998, 143). It is also alleged that many postmodernists are fascinated with technology, do not reject the 'popular' as being beneath them and...[see] publication as a strategic act than a bid for *immortality* (*Ibidem* 144). David Lodge, however, lists five techniques (Lodge, 1977, 228) which may well be said as typical of postmodernist fiction. They are:

(i) *Contradiction*—"Cancels itself out as it goes along" (*Ibid.*, 229);

(ii) *Permutation*—"Alternative narrative lines in the same text" (*Ibid.*, 230);

(iii) *Discontinuity*—"Disrupting the continuity of his discourse by unpredictable swerves of tone, metafictional asides to the reader, blank spaces in the text, contradiction and permutation" (*Ibid.*, 231);

(iv) *Randomness*—"According to a logic of the absurd" (*Ibid.*, 235) and;

(v) *Excess*—"Metaphoric or metonymic devices to excess and testing them to destruction" (*Ibid.*, 235).

These five techniques mentioned above sum up, in essence, what a postmodernist text would be. Linda Hutcheon speaks, almost in a similar fashion, when she refers to "the political dimensions of self-reflexivity, the problematisation of self and history, and the calculated decentering of the text and audience" (Hutcheon, 1988, 218-222) in a postmodern context. In particular, she stresses that the postmodern texts "decode themselves by foregrounding their own contradictions" (*Ibid.*, 211). In a postmodern text, there is a spirit of questioning from within.

One can say that postmodernism is not a fixed system and order but there is an abundance of multiplicity and discontinuity in a postmodernist text. In a postmodernist text, we find the distribution and circulation of the numerous forces and intensities that saturate a text. Postmodernism tends to challenge the traditional humanist belief. Reading into a postmodern framework means looking from a variety of angles *e.g.* as reading a text and by doing this, reading a country. Another major thrust of a postmodern text is that it employs the technique of parody where the powers and conventions of traditional forms and language are subverted; where mimetic art is challenged and changed; where centre and margin keep shifting to the extent that there is a border-blur; where reader becomes the writer and therefore rewrites; where reader is prioritised and; where both the biographic as well as the bibliographic data are inscribed in the text. In essence, postmodernism induces multiple histories, multiple ways of seeing things and does not reduce the reader to one monocentric vision.

Thus, it may do well to understand the various features of postmodernism in the backdrop of a binary structure as a turning away from modernism to *postmodernism;* from objectivity to *self-reflexivity* (looking at yourself; idea of distance between many selves); from universal to *differànce* (differing and defering); from realism to *constructivism* (instead of unmediated way of seeing the world/unadulterated sense of the word, constructivism means that whatever is *real* is constructed); from history to *historiographic perspectivism* (everything becomes different as soon as you read it otherwise, it depends on the experience differently); from language as tools of communication to *language as tools of contamination* (contamination helps it grow, deconstruct); from truth to *blurring of that truth in fiction* (blurring of fact and fiction); from authenticity to *illegitimacy* (one never knows what is real, everything is in a process. It is a legitimate depending on the context. It is not a free flowing thing rather it is like a hall of mirrors); from presence to *absence.* Absence is still a presence. Presence is always shifting. It is not the false idea of being rather it is becoming); from proximity to *duration;* from voice to *heteroglossia* (no monocentric romantic voice but heterogeneous ideas playing simultaneously. Nothing is one's subjective view); from linear time to *temporal shifting* (synchronistic, shifting movement of time); from product to *process;* from centralising to *decentralising* (moving outside of itself, there is an infinite center. Idea of moving away from one meaning); from text to *intertext* (it is not bound by the covers of a book rather the text is connected to a million other book. It is not allusion but the intersection of actual textual forces) and also to *context;* from author-centred to *textual interchange;* from the genre of purity to *border-blur* (the realisation that the distinctions are arbitrarily constructed); from stable subject to a *processual* subject; from topocentric to *tropologic* (Place within the system of language/within the body of the text) and from meaning to *meming* (Meme is a unit of cultural knowledge that replicates itself in language).

II

Arundhati Roy's novel *The God of Small Things* contains all the features of postmodernism which have been delineated in the first section of the paper and very aptly fits into the scheme of a postmodern text, technically speaking, in all senses of the term. According to one interpretation, "In truth, *Small Things* has an easily summarized plot. The setting is an inland town in India's southern state of Kerala in 1969, not so much sultry as dripping with decay, disappointment, family pettiness and social calcification. The main character is Ammu, a divorcee with seven-year-old fraternal twins, who slips into a forbidden love affair just as relatives arrive from distant, admired Britain. A visitor ends up dead, and Ammu's affair leads to tragedy. There are turbulent rivers, unseasonable rains, an interesting peek into the lives of the state's Syrian Christians—a minority with plenty of residual prejudices against India's Hindus—and Big Social Issues, like caste, women's misery and communist politics. *The God of Small Things, i.e.,* social propriety, is the novel's victor. The deity of love and happiness loses out in the end" (Spaeth, 1997, 46).

What is compelling about the novel is the mode of writing, undertaken by Arundhati Roy, which works against an understanding of the way truth, history and power circulate in her text. "The twins were too young to know that these were only history's henchmen. Sent to square the books and collect the dues from those who broke its laws. Impelled by feelings that were primal yet paradoxically wholly impersonal. Feelings of contempt born of inchoate, unacknowledged fear—civilization's fear of nature, men's fear of women, power's fear of powerlessness" (*The God,* 308). Concentrating on the past both as the subject of fiction and as a force of inscribing fiction, the novel traces the ways in which the writer self-consciously participates in the whole construction of the novel.

From "In a purely practical sense it would probably be correct to say that it all began when Sophie Mol came to Ayemenem" (*Ibid.,* 32) to "Little events, ordinary things, smashed and reconstituted. Imbued with new meaning. Suddenly they become the bleached bones of a story" (*Ibid.,* 32-33). We are led to believe in the way construction of the narrative is being made plausible by the novelist. "Still, to say that it all began when Sophie Mol came to Ayemenem is only one way of looking at it" (*Ibid.,* 33). Very apparently declares the self-reflexivity of the novel. This fluidity of the narrative is an important aspect of the novel. The novel is interspersed with a sense of history, with the narrative in a constant fluid condition. The narrative constantly goes back and forth into the narrative space. The entire novel appears to be a constant differing and deferring mode of presentation which is amply evident in the way the novelist is trying very self-reflexively to trace that "the bleached bones of a story" (*Ibid.*, 32) "began when Sophie Mol came to Ayemenem" (*Ibid.*, 32) is but "only one way of looking at it" (*Ibid.*, 33) and "it could be argued that it actually began thousands of years ago" (*Ibid.*, 33) mapping those thousand years with replete references to concrete historical facts, events [Marxists, British, Dutch, Vasco da Gama, Zamorin etc. (*Ibid.*, 33)] and then identifying that "it all began long before Christianity arrived in a boat and seeped into Kerala.... That it really began in the days when the Love Laws were made" (*Ibid.*, 33) ultimately provides a very neat exposition of the brilliantly maneuvered differing and deferring mode of presentation.

The narrative mode of Arundhati Roy is indicated very clearly in the novel when "only one way of looking at it" (*Ibid.*, 33) is discarded and a responsibility is being thrust on the readers to adopt multi-causal multi-centric vision instead of a mono-causal mono-centric vision. This type of narrative mode provides an opportunity for the reader to collaborate with the writer in order to extract meaning out of the text. The lack of any linear narrative, the rejection of representation in favour of self-reference, rejection of the sense of the work of art as an organic whole, rejection of 'character' and 'plot' and finally rejection of meaning itself as a hopeless delusion may be annoying to some readers accustomed to reading traditional novels, but Arundhati Roy shows that whatever appears to be real turns out to be constructed and we hardly have a ready access to what really happened till the very end of the novel. The fluidity of the narrative is imprinted in the novel since the very beginning of the novel when we are told: "And now, twenty three years later their father had re-Returned Estha" (*Ibid.*, 9) and the back and forth movement of the narrative exposing the non-linear progress of it is confirmed within a span of less than two pages in the novel when "After Sophie Mol's funeral, when Estha was Returned, their father sent him to a boy's school in Calcutta" (*Ibid.,* 11) we relapse into the memories of Rahel. Further also, we find it when "It was the first night since she'd come that it hadn't rained. *Around now,* Rahel thought, *if this were Washington, I would be on my way to work. The bus ride. The streetlights. The gas fumes. The shapes of people's breath on the bulletproof glass of my cabin. The clatter of coins pushed towards me in the metal tray. The smell of money on my fingers. The punctual drunk with sober eyes who arrives exactly at ten p.m.: 'Hey, you! Black bitch! suck my dick!'*" (*Ibid.,* 187) which gets back to the point when Rahel is being asked "What are your plans? How long will you be staying? Have you *decided*?" (*Ibid.,* 29). The calculated decentering of the text and audience, which Linda Hutcheon talks about, finds ample expression in the narrative and the novel decodes itself by foregrounding its own contradictions. "Smashed smiles lay ahead of them. But that would be later" (*Ibid.,* 334). "And later become a horrible menacing, goose-bumpy word. Lay. *Ter*" (*Ibid.,* 145). The foregrounding is further reaffirmed when it is said, "as though they knew already that for each tremor of pleasure they would pay with an equal measure of pain" (*Ibid.,* 335).

A beautiful expression of the self-reflexive style of presentation is described in the novel when the three children Rahel, Estha and Sophie Mol are walking, "past the class III Airport Workers' Union token one-day hunger strike. And past the people watching the people" (*Ibid.,* 150-151) and also when "Margaret Kochamma smiled and wagged her rose at him. *Ex-wife, Chacko!* Her lips formed the words, though her voice never spoke them" (*Ibid.,* 142). The back and forth movement of the narrative like "it was an easy-to-understand laugh. Not like the Orangedrink Lemondrink Man's laugh that Estha hadn't understood" (*Ibid.,* 143) is bringing out the fluidity of the narrative. "She was hemmed in by humid hips (as she would be once again, at a funeral in a yellow church) and grim eagerness" (*Ibid.,* 139) provides "alternative lines in the same text" (Lodge, 1977, 230). The parenthesis is not only "disrupting the continuity of [the] discourse by unpredictable swerves of tone [but provides] metafictional asides to the reader" (*Ibid.,* 231). The fluidity of the narrative is evident when Rahel reminisces and the narrative seems to be going backwards (*The God,* 131) to the point where reminiscing stops "Rahel handed Comrade Pillai back the sachet of photographs and tried to *eave*" (*Ibid.,* 134). Thus, the novel seems to be evoking a culture of fragmented sensations. The element of simultaneity—of attachment and detachment, of empathy and distraction—is always a possibility in the novel as in the mingling of the past and present "so that her eyes looked like pink-veined flesh petals (grey in a black and white photograph) (*Ibid.,* 135). The images of simultaneity provide a multi-centric vision of the novel:

> "The performances were staged by the swimming pool. While the drummers drummed and the dancers danced, hotel guests frolicked with their children in the water. While Kunti revealed her secret to Karna on the river bank, courting couples rubbed suntan oil on each other. While fathers played sublimated sexual games with their nubile teenaged daughters, Poothana suckled young Krishna at her poisoned breast. Bhima disemboweled Dushasana and bathed Draupadi's hair in his blood" (*Ibid.,* 127).

The attempts at parodying are not only an act of subversion but they serve in the novel as instruments to provide metafictional aside to the reader foregrounding the contradictions within the structure of the novel:

> Some things come with their own punishments. Like bedrooms with built-in cupboards. They would all learn more about punishments soon. That they came in different sizes. That some were so big they were like cupboards with built-in bedrooms. You could spend your whole life in them wandering through dark shelving (*Ibid.,* 115).

Thus, the novel provides an access to the temporal shifting of time showing the entire exercise of the reading of the novel as a process evoking the readers to read "an absence rather than a presence" (*Ibid.,* 291) thus harping on the constructivism of the novel, "a theoretical construct" (*Ibid.,* 121) reflecting on the historiographic perspectivism "Zamorin's conquest of Calicut...to Love Laws" (*Ibid.,* 33) and "That History used the back verandah to negotiate its terms and collect its *dues*" (*Ibid.,* 199) and "That's the way he was the day History visited them in the back verandah" (*Ibid.,* 190). The novel evokes heteroglossia when we are told:

> The twins, weighed down by their mother's words *If it weren't for you I would be free. I should have dumped you in an orphanage the day you were born. You're the millstones round my neck*—carried nothing (*Ibid.*, 291).

The lines have an echo elsewhere in the novel also:

> 'Because of you!' Ammu had screamed. 'If it wasn't for you I wouldn't be here! None of this would have happened! I wouldn't be here! I would have been free! I should have dumped you in an orphanage the day you were born! You're the millstones round my neck!' (*Ibid.*, 253).

The self-referentiality of the narrative also gives a pointer towards the reading from a marginal point of view referring to mythical "Draupadi (strangely angry only with the men that won her, not the ones that staked her)" (*Ibid.*, 234). Thus, the novel talks about a sense of 'margin-envy' whereby the entire novel becomes self-referential evoking the reader to become writer thus fulfilling the notions of a writerly text. (Barthes) The novelist constantly harps on the idea of an infinite centre which brings forth the idea of moving away from one meaning thus stamping out the possibility of any mono-centric vision. The 'syntactic scissoring' in the novel also aims at the postmodern characteristics of parody. The parody of 'Hello' to 'Hell-oh' in "grown-up's Hello to Margaret Kochamma and a children's Hell-oh to Sophie Mol" (*Ibid.*, 143) and from "Hello, all" (*Ibid.*) to "Hello wall" (*Ibid.*) provides an example of the subversion attempts. The childhood pranks of the fraternal twins as above is further reflected in the form of reading backwards:

> 'ehT serutnevdA fo eisuS lerriuqS. enO gnirps gninrom eisuS lerriuqS ekow pu.' They showed Miss Mitten how it was possible to read both Malayalam and Madam I'm Adam backwards as well as forwards.... She had seen Satan in their eyes. nataS in their seye (*Ibid.*, 60).

The reading backwards evokes this subversive tendency to outwit the imposed western colonial impression. This different-from-the-mirror-image is subversive of Miss Mitten's overtures in the novel who becomes the image of an abhorrent alien whose authority is being questioned. This subversion is more prominent where the novelist shows "an Ambulance that said Sacred Heart Hospital was full of a party of people on their way to a wedding" (*Ibid.,* 60). This subversive style reflects the postcolonial sensibility where the centre-margin, self-other binaries become more and more focussed. It is indeed significant that this kind of reading becomes quite metaphorical in the present text as the whole vision of the novel has that of an advance-and-recoil rhythm *e.g.,* the post-colonial significance of the subversion attempt by welcoming the tourists to the Spice Coast of India to promote tourism where the entire history is embedded in the sign "that said *Kerala Tourism Development Corporation Welcomes You* with a Kathakali dancer doing a namaste. Another sign, unwobbled by a kangaroo, said: emocleW ot eht ecipS tsaoC fo aidnI" (*Ibid.,* 139).

The language of the novel is mutilated to the effect that the contamination helps it grow. The author is able to create a tension with the meaningful punctuational order and italics which works as a statemental index to the critical tension which looms large over the fictional world of Arundhati Roy from It had been the *What Will Sophie Mol Think?* week (*Ibid.,* 36) to "swimming across was not the problem. Taking the boat with Things in it (so that they could (be) Prepare to prepare to be prepared) *was*" (*Ibid.,* 204). The entire novel is marked with the intermittent use of full points and question marks along with cryptic, incisive, italic statemental authorial interventions. The words, and sometimes lines, sound horrid when repeated, evoking the most sterile, machine-like reverberation of life-minus-life:

> 'Imagine. It's still here. I stole it. After you were Returned.' That word slipped out easily. *Returned.* As though that was what twins were meant for. To be borrowed and returned. Like library books (*Ibid.,* 156).

The use of the language also provides a whole set of binary oppositions creating the images of violence as verbal constructs. The formidable nature of violence and an elaborate account of the hidden form of violence are noticeable:

> Unlike the custom of rampaging religious mobs or conquering armies running riot, that morning in the Heart of Darkness the posse of Touchable Policemen acted with

> economy, not frenzy. Efficiency, not anarchy. Responsibility, not hysteria. They didn't tear out his hair or burn him alive. They didn't hack off his genitals and stuff them in his mouth. They didn't rape him. Or behead him. After all, they were not battling an epidemic. They were merely inoculating a community against an outbreak (*Ibid.*, 309).

or pathos

> '*Bye, Estha. Godbless,* Ammu's mouth had said. Ammu's trying-not-to-cry mouth' (*Ibid.*, 300).

Similarly, use of deviations like 'Nevertheless' has been used by the novelist to expand the horizons of the readers. Every time it is introduced in the novel, it invites the reader to put in their point of view in reading. The Derridean idea that a text is a gas and as such has so much of energy that it can create wide horizons for the readers is very well reflected in 'Nevertheless, my dear,' Chacko said in his Reading Aloud voice. 'Never. The. Less' (*Ibid.*, 55) or the use of *locus standi,* in the sense of the swarming image of locusts out to usurp when "Chacko told Rahel and Estha that Ayemenem had no locusts stand I." It not only subverts the language eventually expanding the horizons of readers' mind by referring to the phallocentric disdain towards the marginalised gender but also forms a protest against the use of the non-English word *locus standi* or the use of five numbers of yes together to show the "nod in mass consent. Yesyesyesyesyes" (*Ibid.*, 86).

The foregrounding of narrative's contradiction helps it cancel itself as it goes along. "Esthappen Yako finished his free bottle of fizzed, lemon-flavoured fear. His lemontoolemon, too cold. Too sweet. The fizz came up his nose. He would be given another bottle soon (free, fizzed fear)" (*Ibid.*, 105) shows that the reader is being prioritized and provides only as an example of teasing of the reader for collaboration with the novelist. The narrative-into-a-narrative pattern falls into the broad framework of a postmodern text which *The God of Small Things* proves to be:

> "And there was Captain von Clapp-Trapp. Christopher Plummer. Arrogant. Hardhearted. With a mouth like a slit. And a steel shrill police whistle. A captain with seven children. Clean children, like a packet of peppermints. He

> pretended not to love them, but he did. He loved them. He loved her (Julie Andrews), she loved him, they loved the children, the children loved them. They all loved each other. They were clean, white children, and their beds were soft with Ei. Der. Downs" (*Ibid.,* 105).

The blurring of the past, future & present tense gives us another example of simultaneousness or multiplicity:

> When long bus journeys, and overnight stays at the airport, were met by love and a look of shame, small cracks appeared, which would grow and grow, and before they knew it, the Foreign Returnees would be trapped outside the History House, and have their dreams redreamed (*Ibid.,* 140-141).

The emergence of the text as an imminently processual subject, where the final product is not the thing which is being emphasised most, leads to the realization that the text is not bound by the covers of a book as it is connected and intersected with several other books. This textual interchange is not allusion in the strict sense of the term rather an intersection of actual textual forces. The element of intertextuality, however, provides a method of projecting a link between past and present, antiquity and contemporaneity and other binaries eventually helping the reader delve deeper into the eclecticism of Arundhati Roy's fictional world. While the priest with curly beards swung pots of frankincense on chains and never smiled at babies the way they did on usual Sundays (*Ibid.,* 4) reminds us of Blakian disgust with the ecclesiatical authority, Keatsian "season of mists and mellow fruitfulness" is contrasted in Ayemenem's world marked by "shrinking river and vacuous humming" (*Ibid.,* 1). Similarly "a hot breeding month" of "May in Ayemenem" (*Ibid.,* 1) immediately reminds the audience of similar references to a particular month of a Calendar in the form of description of April reflected in celebration of the spring exuberance and the unitive vision of Chaucer and destructive decayed and dehumanized vision of T.S. Eliot in 'Whanne that Aprille with its showers soote' to 'April is the cruellest month' of Chaucer and Eliot's world respectively. The notion of intertextuality finds ample expression in the novel and fits it into the paradigm of a postmodern text.

Summing up, Arundhati Roy's *The God of Small Things* evokes "a culture of fragmentary sensations, eclectic nostalgia, disposable simulacra and promiscuous superficiality" by harping on the idea of an infinite centre which brings forth the idea of moving away from a particular, one meaning. Crucially, the novel also provides an intriguingly hermeneutic experience by withholding something significant from the reader who has to look intently into the woofings and warpings of the texture in order to attain the knowledge of that elusive 'truth.' The novel is, in fact, an example of miming instead of meaning, which has been rejected as a hopeless delusion, as so many things are gleamed through it. As a unit of cultural knowledge, mime replicates itself in language and a bunch of information is passed on to the reader evoking a big information system through which the novelist or the writer is able to communicate whole range of thoughts from "a male chauvinist society (*Ibid.*, 57) to a patriarchal mode of appropriation of women's rights where "What's yours is mine and what's mine is also mine" (*Ibid.*) to "the Walking Backwards days torn between Loyalty and Love" (*Ibid.*, 255) to the "feelings of contempt born of inchoate, unacknowledged fear—civilization's fear of nature, men's fear of women, power's fear of powerlessness" (*Ibid.*, 308) and leads to aspects of a more general human condition in the late capitalist postmodern world of today.

WORKS CITED

Barthes, Roland, 1990, *S/Z.* Miller, Richard (trans.) Oxford: Blackwell.

Harvey, David, 1989, The Condition of *Postmodernity.* Oxford: Blackwell.

Hassan, Ihab, 1985, "A Culture of Postmodernism," *Theory, Culture and Society.* 2(3), 119-31.

Hawthorn, Jeremy, 1998, *A Concise Glossary of Contemporary Literary Theory.* London: Arnold.

Hutcheon, Linda, 1988, *A Poetics of Postmodernism: History, Theory, Fiction.* London: Routledge.

Huyssen, Andreas, 1988, *After the Great Divide: Modernism, Mass Culture and Postmodernism.* London: Macmillan.

Lodge, David, 1977, *The Modes of Modern Writing: Metaphor, Metonymy, and the Typology of Modern Literature.* London: Arnold.

Roy, Arundhati, 1997, *The God of Small Things.* New Delhi: IndiaInk.

Spaeth, Antony, 1997, "No Small Thing," *TIME.* April 14: 46-47.

13

RAJA RAO'S *COMRADE KIRILLOV*: A CRITICAL APPRAISAL

KAVITA AGRAWAL

In Raja Rao's fourth novel *Comrade Kirillov* there is a fine synthesis of tradition and modernity and an intellectual perspective revealing the varied impacts of the contact between the East and the West. The great literary *Sadhak* has combined the different cultures and thoughts with respective meanings, scopes, importance in life, and their impact on each other that provide the real theme of the novel. He thinks that both cultures of the East and the West are like red and white corpuscles in human blood. They are antagonistic yet they are essential components of the flow of life. We can not avoid the traditions of our ancient cultures and we can also not survive by neglecting our modern social patterns of the West. We have to collect the flowers of both cultures to make a beautiful garland of our choice.

Comrade Kirillov is the story of a divided mind. In the novel the inward conflict operates on an altogether different dimension, of the divided consciousness of a man torn between two pulls. A complex of ideas, generated by the protagonist's conscious 'intellectual conviction and commitment' on the one hand and his sub-conscious attitude about his emotional leanings on the other constitute the fabric of the thematic development of the novel. Obviously, the central subject in the *Comrade Kirillov* is the situation of the divided consciousness caused by a double commitment—rational and emotional or conscious and unconscious. What probably is hinted at is the fact that communism—an ideology of occidental origin can win the mind of an oriental traditionalist but not his heart, producing inevitably a dilemma of the divided mind.[1] "The protagonist is an "Inverted Brahmin."[2] He is a Marxist and has placed the material ends of life over the spiritual level. He remains a simple and unified personality but the sway of an alien ideology over his mind brings all the complexity in his character. His real name is Padmanabha Iyer. He belongs to the South Indian Brahmin family, but he wore a necktie which had a "prater plus parenthetical."[3] He is the combination of the Eastern Brahmin-culture and the Western rational and inquisitive mind. He is a Brahmin by heart but has changed an anti-Brahmin outside. Nevertheless the novelist wants to say that Padmanath Iyer (Comrade Kirillov) remains a Brahmin, suffering, no doubt, from a conflict between honesty of mind—the intellectual loyalty to Marxism—and honesty of being—the emotional pulls being a Hindu.

He was a Brahmin and a South Indian. He started to receive his earlier schooling and higher education in India. He came under the bewitching influence of Theosophy, which took him westward "Proselytizing flood."[4] The protagonist has his Indian traditional dress. The novelist has given a humorous description of his personality. He wore a strange type of pant, a flapping little coat. His strange type of rounded muscles and lip make his personality a humorous one. Kirillov was an Indian, his pants too dissimilar his limbs, his coat flapping a little too fatherly on his small, rounded muscles of seating, his lip tender, slow and segregate—out of which eked true words of numbers, which his narrow, dun eyes gave an added touch of humanity to his ancient and enigmatic face.

It would seem as though, seated on his barrel—which, he soon explained, did the service of economy and of convenience, as its roundless made rotation easier, its height made the table come nearer his bust, and besides, it gave the only chair in his large, furniture—lorn flat the gracious emptiness which could soothen the seating of comrades, and even be kind to a heathen like him—seated on his ground, full barrel, it would seem as if, searching for a word, he had pushed him check muscles upwards, yet upwards, which gave him the necessary Mongoloid look. The desire of this world discovery. The master was indeed there, and born, but he was too adolescent for his prophetic destiny, time and theosophical workings would ultimately reveal the messiah. So it was in this messianic awaiting that Kirillov first set his foot on the American soil. The great Mother of mankind was far away, sequestered and adept in Tibetan mysteries, to whom the glow of the Final-incarnate would be revealed soon, very soon, and amidst a thousand lotus-petal opals. Truth and virginity are of high historical demand—and grace and beauty must dance to a holied world.[5]

Mr. Iyer was a man of refined taste. He wanted to enrich his knowledge, therefore, he was driven into the intellectual world of hope. He began to think seriously about the good books on different subjects. He got books of all kind and specially the social books. He heard that England was the home of learning and therefore, he had a keen desire to go there and use his intelligence by joining the Lllllllabour party. He was also told that Germany and France were also the great centres of learning. So he learnt German in order to read Fourier and Saint Simon and he was gradually pushed towards Lenin. Engel seemed to him a very machine of monumental and systematized thought and the Russian Revolution was a remarkable experiment; it was the only historic revelation of the modern world. The protagonist now changed his name as Comrade Kirillov. On one summer morning of 1928 he went to Liverpool. He had a small luggage but had a number of books of his best choice. He took on rent a hotel in Greek street of the city. It was a vegetarian restaurant. Unlike his fellow South Indians he had very small diet. He was much interested in the Labour party and his newspapers of England. He knew about the elections of the Labour party. He studied deeply about the laws and regulations of the Labour party. He was much attracted the veracity of Karl Marx. Previously he was much interested in the Theosophy Society and Mahatma Gandhi. He was attracted toward Mrs Annie Besant and her ideals. She was an Irish origin.

Annie Besant, first of all was drawn early into the Fabian movement, but she soon discovered Theosophy through Madame Blavatsky, and became its President. She settled in Adyar, and fought for Indian Home-rule, as it was then called, and even became for one year the President of the Indian

National Congress. It was she who discovered the spiritual greatness of Krishnamurti and organized an international society—the order of the Star in the East—in preparation for the emergence of this new Messiah. She also chose many young men to be his future companions, for when Krishnamurti would realize in full of his own spiritual destiny. The members of Theosophical Society considered him as their "Messiah."[6]

> Kirillov, was pining among thirsty souls for the vision of the messiah, but time led him to more busy meditations. The destiny of India was deeply bound with the outcome of theosophy, and Mrs Annie Besant was the great Indian patriot, whose peregrinations across the thundering world would cause India to emerge out of the mess of Anglo-Saxon devilry and create a double movement of freedom and prophetic dominion. The wicked English would go, the great Master of the human race, now born, and already being prepared for his historic mission, would reveal the real India to be. Here for once, since the days of the great incarnations. And the seven wise men of the West would bring their magian offerings to the child of holy, Benares. And five would be his favourite disciples, like with the great Galilean, and Kirillov would be one of them.[7]

Kirillov came to Communism via theosophy. His real conversion took place when he became a communist and in that conversion lay a veritable reincarnation. Padmanabha Iyer became Kirillov, creating an ambivalence in his own character and mind. This ambivalence of the mind of a spirited convert is ironically reflected in the tie he wore. His journey continues from India. He went to California and then went to London, followed in the end to Moscow and Peking. He was thirsty for knowledge and was searching for reality. But he was not satisfied. America, England and Russia could not satisfy him. India was always in his mind, because it is a great ocean of knowledge and therefore, he could not completely alienate himself from his birthplace. As a seeker of knowledge the protagonist throughout his journey scatters across his gems of thoughts on various subjects like dialectics, Communism, History, Theosophy, Sex and love-making, Gandhism, education as it is in India, democracy, etc. Which are not only-revealing but really constitute the main contexture of the novel. The novelist has given his remarkable views on theosophy in the following words:

> In Adyar, theosophy explained Karma, and the limbs and height thus revealed a past life history, yet your soul could still rise to deva-heights. Man was born for brightness and the light of the Adepts and Masters shone on the growing sixth human sub-race. The new age will soon be upon us, and intelligence can take you a long way in the discovery of cosmic mystery. If you meditate this way, you rise three stages in seven years, but this other way may make you see extraordinary inter-terrestrial lights, bright blue or tertian-yellow. They can only be seen with especial eyes, and for this you need much dieting and breath training. In the comforts thus of the deva world you could lead a bright earthly life and, when wanted, switch on to a heavenly one. Besides, you could see Masters (deep set in the Himalayan snows) whose luminescence would give you fatherly care and noble guidance.[8]

Raja Roy has also given the sub-title of the novel as "A New Novel." The second title is most appropriate to the novel because "it is new mainly in its employment of the structural device of irony which adds force and fullness to its narrative. The large-scale use of irony in the narrative technique saves it from being a mere catalogues of the strength and weaknesses of Communism and also saves the characterization of the protagonist from degrading into caricature. It also prepares the ground for the revelation of the duality in Kirillov's character. Possibilities and limitations of Communism are laid bare before us through the dialogues between the narrator and the protagonist as much as through the ironic details of the ideology. Irony sustains the double voice of the narrative, articulating simultaneously the indefatigable logic, of Communism and its limitations through an implicit criticism of its tenets."[9]

The novelist in the novel rightly says:

> The Messiah was not only born—he worked, and his land was called the union of the Soviet Socialist Republics, and may be a new Ganges flowed there, and man there had all the prismatic colours of the prophetic world. Besides, it was built on reason and its steam engine.[10]

Comrade Kirillov now became a complete Communist. From his original name he adopted his second name Kirillov. It created an ambivalence in his own character and mind. This ambivalence of the mind of a spirited convert is ironically reflected in the tie he wore. This new conversion had given strange ascetic incision to his Brahminic manner. He had high and bright hopes for his future life. He believed that Communism would usher in a state of society where no man would be master of another, and where a man like him would sit on some lone hilltop and would write beautiful books, instead of wandering in search of metaphysical will-of-the wisp, and a cup of coffee. But later on, he came to know that it was not so as he thought. It revealed that the individual in a Communistic society is just a biological number—an anonymous entity. The interest lies not so much in the common places of a communistic credo as in the ironic details of Kirillov's prepared speech, which he poured out like a snake charmer playing upon his bamboo flute:

> If the biology of selective killing were understood, humanity might yet attain the clean apex of history. There, you build the point of the pyramid, and under it through the mystic cave door you bring in processional the treasures of the three worlds. You have all the deserts in golden perspective, and the Nile flows in chartered movements to a mellow sea.... Death, the Moscow deaths, were the antiseptics of history—you kill for the beauty of your eyes.[11]

At New York Kirillov was busy in study a large number of books, which converted his mind. He was a good and fast reader. On the basis of books he began to hold a lengthy discourse on dialectics, participated in Labour party meetings and it was on the benches of the Bloomsbury Parks that he found the veracity of Karl Marx. Now he began to work for publishers according to their demands he began to translate books. His interest began to arise in translating the books of his own choice also. The left-wing publishers with a selective and universal outlook had a particular fascination for him. He was turning away from Theosophy and Gandhism and found in Communism a retreat where he could receive his heart's desire.

> It was the time of Second World War. Hitler was creating havoc. London was facing a terrible situation. The city of London was bombed constantly by the bombs of Hitler. Stalin in the beginning of the war stood mightily behind Hitler. The world was turning a new leaf so far as its ideologies, geographies, shapes and colours were concerned.
>
> Hitlerian bombs poured gleefully on London, and in the darkness the violet and the rose, the blue and the yellow, spattered with such confident carelessness. You must spit colour— and it falleth where it willeth—burn, burn, you bloody city. Your magnificence has too long towards but on the other tithes and deaths. Hitler seemed almost an archangel, and his fire had communist ire. Stalin stood mightily behind Hitler—with the backing of the Russian bear the world could be steam rollered.[12]

The protagonist was in a romantic mood and in the mean time he fell in love with a young Czech girl. Her name was Irene. She was very beautiful and charming girl. She was a sincere, educated and reasonable girl. Soon Comrade Kirillov married her. The protagonist was very happy in this changing world of ideologies, geographies, shapes and colours. "Kirillov really loved Irene. She had the red blood, the red hair, the passionate index figure and dialectics had drained her lust into irate channels. Her duty was to be faithful to this man, and fight for the party. At once this bloody war was over, the arch of freedom would span the sky from Czechoslovakia to India—why from Greenland to Indonesia. She made Kirillov nice, rich spiced tea, prepared his break! and cheese for the British Museum, and when evening came, she returned always at five from her classes (at the London School of Economics) so that Kirillov should not miss a warm meal. She set by him with the kindest of smiles as he ruminated over same abstruse economic indignity in the plantations of Jamaica, or admits the tribal populations of the Marshal Islands."[13] She was a very faithful and sincere wife. She was always worried about his health. She was the best nurse for him. After some time she became pregnant and gave birth to a male child. The child was a wonderful boy. His father was an Indian and a Czech mother. He was given the name as Kamal. In the war, India was taking the favour of British government. The protagonist got a party directive, which emphasized "toeing the British line."

"Since this was a people's war, India was on the right side, the British side, and he who spoke against them sold himself to the enemy. Kirillov lay wondering at the instructions received from Stalin. He could simply close his eyes and go into profound meditation, seeking the meaning of event and statistic to their dialectical finality. If Stalin had asked India to side with the British, Stalin had a definite logical construction on which to base his conclusions. Kirillov wandered into himself and those were very painful days indeed, the murkiest he had ever known. Coming out of his 'Sommal Psychosis' (his own words) he sat down one morning and wrote a brilliant thesis on the subject. He was inspired like a poet on the subject and his arguments came easily and learnedly. He wrote it all down and looked at his wife sweetness for the first time. A short of inner conversion was brought out in him, which, he felt, seemed to have changed his skin. Stalin had made him white and the Indian struggle entered the international arena and he now suddenly could see the skin of Irene on his own wrist and hand, as if by divine compassion."[14]

The protagonist began to increase his reputation. He was also invited by the British council to varied assemblies and Kirillov developed astonishing labour theories on the people's war before his receptive audiences. Now he became a prominent authority. He stamped his name in the international history. 1942 brought with it the great Indian revolution, which shook Churchill and British prolonged her commitments for another four years. The journey of protagonist from India to California and then to London followed to Moscow and Peking increased his gradual knowledge of a number of fundamental philosophical thoughts. He was attracted by the noble deeds of Mahatma Gandhi and so he wrote a book with the title "Mahatma Gandhi—A Marxist Interpretation." In this book he has given his some memorable remarks on the two great men of the age—Marx and Mahatma Gandhi.

Marx's unDarwinian enemy was "this Mahatma Gandhi, friend and fool of the poor, the Sadhu reactionary who still believed in caste and creed and such categories and whose birth in this world had set history many centuries backwards.

Marx indeed built in his theory of revolution on the British working classes revolting against their mastery, heralded by the rising in the vast dominion of the British Crown called India— and Mahatma Gandhi came and upset Marx. If Marx were alive no doubt Mahatma Gandhi would have received, under the mighty pen of the great Master, the destiny he deserved. Gandhi was somewhat of an oriental Mazzini, with India mysticism to boot. Much like Mazzini this new prophet of God had the Almighty too often on his lips...non-violence was a biological lie. Man was born to fight—fighting is an instrument of Darwinian evolution, which made dialectics possible."[15] Without opposition there can be no progress. His sympathies were with China. He possessed great faith and feeling for this country. He was a Communist through and through and had no faith in Gandhism:

> During the Hitler war—I was in India then—I often wondered whether war had not made his dark skin darker, and standing on some rubbish heap, would he not have gazed and gazed at the righteous sky which poured such magnificent fire on the Beelzebuty city? The new Jerusalem was up the road, down the valley of pillared destruction and the sinuous sins of the Champs Elysees, through Poland and Bessarabia to a united Mayday demonstration of an Indian Kremlin. The Chinese would be marching in newly discovered enthusiasm—Kirillov had great faith and feeling for China—and the ragged Indian would march behind, humiliated by the military magnificence of the Soviet Army. Mahatma Gandhi would be dead—and wish to God it would be soon—and the Nehru-Patel clique liquidated, as Kerensky was.[16]

In the novel Raja Rao has given his opinion that Islam is the staunchest supporter of British defense. But the Hindus had always been the mysterious oriental to the Britisher. Comrade Kirillov took place far away from India to the Western countries where most of his life was spent. But he was born in India and his upbringing was also in his country. All these two factors had a strong and firm hold on him. In the beginning he was a Theosophist and later on turned Communist or Marxist. This became a powerful and deep impact upon his life. But he was the child of India, where as long as Lord

Shiva is in Kailash and the holy Ganga flows from his hair, Indians will not betray their land. It is the culture of India that the motherland is much bigger than all politics, all economics, all castes, and all philosophies. Comrade Kirillov, in spite of his Western thoughts was almost a child of his country, unfortunately, for some reasons he was caught in the mighty ideological contradictions of the modern world and torn between his intellectual and emotional pulls. Spiritually he is attached to Indian spirit but physically he is with Western philosophy. He adores what is noble and good in the Indian thought irrelevant, obsolete and antediluvian in it. Gandhism and Communism, the two are poles apart in their thinking and non-violence was a biological lie. Moreover, Mahatma Gandhi was Kleptomaniac.

> ...Your Gandhi is a Kleptomaniac. You know what Kleptomania is. It is the instinct for stealing money from others. You can read any day in the provincial newspapers of this country in Juvenile courts. The fact is Mahatma Gandhi is an ungrown adult. Look at his theories on sex—he justifies the sexual act in terms of theological necessities: God wanted to people the world. When he wants the population to rise, then you know it instinctively. You feel like increasing the population of your own home. Then you can go to the bed with your wife and produce the prescribed number of fetuses for population figures. Otherwise, you impose sisterhood on your young wife, and spread a carpet of virtue between you and your spouse. Fine, very fine counsels in this age of reason. Ask your Gandhi to read Freud—he would be the wiser for it.[17]

Kirillov thinks that Gandhi would be a wiser man if he read the psychology of Freud. He could almost speak of India as though he was talking of a venerable old lady in a fairy who had nothing but goodness in the heart and who was made of morning dew and mountain honey. Like *The Serpent and the Rope,* another major work of Raja Rao, Comrade Kirillov is essentially a spiritual autobiography. The novelist Raja Rao, is himself the storyteller of his novel *Comrade Kirillov.* The novelist tells almost his own story in a modified way and tries to find out the truth by putting chronological events. The diary of the heroine, Irene is also important. He uses important quotations and tales from the Upanishads and the Vedas to discuss the philosophical and political systems. The hero of the novel and the novelist both closely resemble to each other. They have their spiritual quest for truth. They want to unfold of a Vedanta-based vision of India and deals with the magnitude, mystery, complexity, philosophy and metaphysics of India along with that of the West from the point of view of one who seeks Brahman and whose sensibility and values are uncompromisingly Indian. The novelist belongs to an ancient Brahmin family. Vidyaranya Swami, who was the greatest teacher of Advaita after Shankara, was his illustrious ancestor. Even his grandfather was a remarkable scholar, the novelist himself was a university wit. He had higher and good education at the Nizam College, Hydrabad and Aligarh University, Aligarh. Moreover he had also studied at Montpellier and at the Sorbonne. But he was always an Indian. Even when he went to North Africa, he carried the message of Ramakrishana. A story feeling of Indian social movement was in his blood. He was feeling that a strong pro-socialist movement is shaping a new India and will triumph there in spite of bigotry.

The novelist's marriage with Camille Mouly at Montpellier University, changed his life. This marriage remained for ten years (1937-1947). Though she was a foreign woman but her heart was almost of a Hindu. She had great regard for Hinduism and Kannada and she made sincere efforts to live like a Hindu. She inspired Raja Rao to write in both English and French. Though Raja Rao virtually settled down in France, he never lost his contact with the land of his birth and he discovered India only after going abroad. He realized the truth in his country's culture and he vitalized his inner resources with his country's traditional values. So when he returned back to India his activities in India were not only confined to visiting ashrams but also participating in underground activities of the young social and spiritual leaders.

In 1943 when he came to India, he met a great sage, Atmananda Guru, and he discovered answers to all of his questions and his quest seems to be over. He remained in India for sixteen years and enriched his spiritual knowledge in touch with his Guru. But after the death of his Guru in

1959 he went again to France and began to deliver his lectures on Indian philosophy at the University of Texas. His contact with an American stage actress named Katherine Jones, converted into a love, which later on turned into a second marriage with her. The lady gave birth to a son named Christopher Rama. His very name was the combination of the cultures of the two countries (France and India). All these autobiographical glimpses and novelist's thoughts we find in his third novel *The Cat and the Shakespeare* (1965) and *Comrade Kirillov*.

We find that the novelist had many points of resemblance between their (protagonists) life and temperament both. Comrade Kirillov is, to a considerable extent, a copy of Raja Rao. Comrade Kirillov has been all alone an ardent lover and reader of books. We find that the novelist as well as the protagonist of the novel *Comrade Kirillov* spent most of their time in reading books. Both had been one of the dominating passions of their lives. His life like the life of the novelist had been a persistent quest for truth and he is heir to the two worlds. These, two worlds in his life had great importance. His first world was of his birth and parentage while the second world was where he had passed the major portion of his adult life. He has been influenced by the best in both Eastern and Western thoughts. His debt to the West is considerable, but his sensibility has remained Indian to the core. Like Comrade Kirillov, the novelist had also close relations with the socialist movement in Paris.

Comrade Kirillov is the novel of a very simple story. It is very straightforward. But its thought is very compact. The critics do not consider it a proper novel. They consider it a "novelette." It has hardly one hundred and thirty two pages in small size. Description is reduced to the barest minimum. The whole story rotates only on one character. It is intended to analyse of the mind of one character, which is Comrade Kirillov, and the whole of the novelist's attention is focussed absolutely on the evolution of his mind. The novelist has given no chapter wise divisions of the novel. There is only one mark of division on page fifty, just near about halfway in the novel. "Irene's Diary" is introduced on page 94. It dates from July 4, 1944 to January 4, 1949. This diary is significant from two points of view: one, it reveals the character and personality of Comrade Kirillov, as Irene sees it, and two, it lets us into her own mind viscous-a-viscous Comrade Kirillov. It also causes a second demarcation of construction of the plot in the novel. The novel contains brief notes at the end for the use of the readers. The plot does not follow a chronological sequence of time and place, although semblance of it is maintained to sustain interest. The method adopted is more of suggestion, for what else could be done in a small compass like this, and of analysis of motives and opinions than of elaborate and full-length descriptions. The novel may be regarded truly as a minor Indian classic both in its theme and treatment. The manner in which it is written is entirely author's own. Sometimes the continual philosophic digressions and dialectics are irritating, but what make the book worth reading nevertheless are its philosophizing, its quotations from Sanskrit and its references to the myths and traditions of India. And the comparisons and contrasts implicit in the different forms of pairs of faiths serve to emphasize that India is not a country, "like France is, or like England, India is an idea, a metaphysic."[18]

The narrator of the novel is Raja Rao himself who has presented the metaphysical talks in the novel. The story is very thin based on the thoughts of the protagonist. The main character is Comrade Kirillov. The other characters are Irene, his wife, Kamal his son and the storyteller the novelist himself. They are all static and flat. They do not make any growth nor they are dynamic. The whole story rotates on the Comrade Kirillov's mind from Theosophy to Communism, and the conflicts he faces in the context, heart-burnings and headaches they involve, but it is not so much as a man of flesh and blood that he emerges before us, as the embodiment of an idea. The protagonist demands a highly intellectual, well-read and patient category of readers for its full appreciation. The novel faces the problem of multi-facet activities of life.

The readers get only some insight into the implied author's personal views as well as do gleam an idea of his skill in handling first person narrator's either remotely or intimately identified with him by a close examination of tone, selection of details, and characterization. Comrade Kirillov has his full faith that in a Communist state there will be society where no man will be master of another:

> If the biology of selective killing were understood, humanity might yet attain the clean apex of history. There, you build the point of the pyramid, and it through the mystic cave door you bring in processional the treasures of the three worlds. You have all the deserts in golden perspective, and the Nile flows in charted movements to a mellow sea.... Death, the Moscow deaths, were the antiseptics of history—you kill for the beauty of the ages.[19]

The story of protagonist is full of ironic views. He had simplified his faith in material progress as the highest norm of a happy life. The novelist has used double-edged irony in the novel. He cuts both ways making a well-aimed attack on Communism on the one hand and criticizing decadent Hinduism or imperialistic British on the other. The novelist attacks on the evils of profiteering capitalism. His denigration of Hinduism is not altogether free from irony. He expresses the condemnation of the feelings of Hinduism in his famous religious novel *The Serpent and the Rope:*

> Indeed, the most reactionary force in world politics today—far more poisonous that Chiang Kai Shek—is your Hindu. He and his metaphysical myths, his Karma and his caste, his I-will-not-eat this and I will-not-touch-that, his superior feelings and his importance—his decadence is the foulest our earth has to bear.[20]

Raja Rao is a great thinker who has history at his beck and call to support his viewpoint. As a philosopher of history he depicts in *Comrade Kirillov* a phase of contemporary Indian history in which one finds the intellectuals torn between divergent pulls of two ways of life. The protagonist embodies through his own inward conflict the fight between a radical progressive and an ort odox traditionalist, each coexists with the other in the self of a modernized enlightened Brahmin like the novelist who is equally sensitive to both though unyielding to totalitarian progressivism of a communist society. In the novel there is a great conflict between traditional rooted morality and Western intellectual convictions. They create "existential melancholy"[21] in the protagonist. He is highly confident and optimistic in his hopes and ambitions. His communistic character is brought into relief bit by bit:

> One wonders how much Stalin's confidence did not sustain and reassure Roosevelt. The Churchillian resources are on the verbal side—Stalin creates the worlds of his willing. Roosevelt must, at moments, have almost envied, and perhaps worshipped his communist colleague. Churchill, the fighting cock could blow the loudest Marlborough trumpet.[22]

In the Second World War the protagonist was welcomed by the Britishers. But it is a matter of ridicule that in spite of a Communist he was not a diehard rationalist. Red colour was very dear to him. It is the colour of the Communist. He loved his wife very much. The reason was that she had the red blood, the red hair, the passionate index finger, and dialectics had drained her lust into irate channels. Her comradely duty was to be faithful to this man, and fight for the party. His wife's diary is very important because it reveals so many important points and illustrates Comrade Kirillov's defense of Communist ideology as well as his love for Gandhi and India as also the inner tension that he felt on account of the inherent conflict between the two. He lives in on grave tensions. His diary makes the readers aware of the protagonist's inward conflict, which was only partly revealed in the main part of the novel. It makes the novel a powerful character study and adds to it a psychological focus. The conflict he is tormented with is between the assertive idealism and inborn emotionalism. We find the combination of poetical Indian traditional and Western impact in his character:

> ...Kirillov was an Indian, and he had peculiar reactions, which no dialectics could clarify. He could almost speak of India as though he were talking of a venerable old lady in a fairy tale who had nothing but goodness in her heart and who was made of morning dew and mountain honey.[23]

As a staunch and true Communist he describes Mahatma Gandhi as an "ungrown adult." He considers him that he should have been born in the middle ages. Even then his language is milder one for this Indian saint Churchill had used more bitter words against this saintly Indian leader. We find him as "a divided mind" because he hates the Muslims and the British as a Hindu nationalist and defends and admires Muslims and the British as a Hindu nationalist:

> You brag about progress and remain a vegetarian. You brag about Islam and Communism and call your son Kamal Dev instead of calling him Stephanovich, or Electricity, as in the earlier days of the revolution. And when you wake up in the morning in your bed; I am sure you remember your mother's instructions: open your hands, and say the verse, hasta-Kamal, etc. you are an old hypocrite, I am sure, and an unrepentant one.[24]

The whole novel is centered with the character and activities of Mr. Padmanabhan, Kirillov. "Kirillov starts as a seeker of truth, but after becoming a Communist, he is increasingly revealed by the narrator to be caught in a system which curtails his access of truth. Thus, Kirillov continuously rationalizes the major events in the world to suit his perspective. Nevertheless, following a visit to India several years after he has left, he realizes that his Communism is only a thin upper layer in an essentially Indian Psyche. Irene also recognizes in her diary that he is almost biologically an Indian Brahmin and only intellectually a Marxist."[25] Throughout the novel we find that his story is of a divided mind. The novelist has shown him to be a man of contradictions: attacking and worshipping Gandhi simultaneously, deeply loving traditional Indian but campaigning for a Communist revolution reciting Sanskrit shlokes but professing communism. Raja Rao is his protagonist's intellectual opposite. He is an adherent of Advaita Vedanta. His relation with his wife Irene recalls Rama's relationship with Madeleine. The couple is blessed with a son, Kamal. Soon after his return from India, his wife dies in childbirth, followed by her newly born daughter. He leaves for Moscow and is last heard in Beijing the narrator of the story takes Kamal to Kanyakumari and where he joins his grandparent's place.

The holy place of Kanyakumari becomes identified with Parvati, the Eternal Virgin. The character of the protagonist becomes a mystic. "Irene sees only the inveterate Indian in him, while (Raja Rao) sees him sold over to an alien ideology. But Iyer himself perhaps feels caught between contradictory pulls, orthodoxy and modernism, Gandhism and Communism, inner certitude and outer frenzy, and is leap into East Europe a gesture of despair, or a Hope for the future? As in *The Serpent and the Rope,* in Comrade Kirillov also Raja Rao's deeper intention seems to be to show that, for an Indian, 'holy wedded love' is impossible with a European wife however unexceptionable otherwise; and again, an Indian's attempt to forge a life of fulfilment outside the motherland is foredoomed to failure, whatever the other attractions and inducements of the adopted country."[26]

Thus *Comrade Kirillov* presents India's traditional sublime views through the main characters of the novel; but side by side Raja Rao does not ignore the modern progressive views and ideologies of the some philosophers and scholars of the West. He has synthesized tradition and modernity in a fine way.

NOTES AND REFERENCES

1. Srivastava Narsingh, *The Mind and Art of Raja Rao* (Barreilly, Prakash Book Depot, 1980), 92.
2. Raja Rao, *Comrade Kirillov*: (New Delhi, Orient Paperbooks. 1976), 119.
3. *Ibid.*, 120.
4. *Ibid.*, 7-8.
5. *Ibid.*, 8-9.
6. *Ibid.*, 14.
7. *Ibid.*, 9-10.
8. *Ibid.*, 12-13.
9. Srivastava Narsingh, *The Mind and Art of Raja Rao* (Barreilly, Prakash Book Depot, 1980), 15.
10. Raja Rao, *Comrade Kirillov* (New Delhi, Orient Paperbooks, 1976), 46.
11. *Ibid.*, 46.
12. *Ibid.*, 54.
13. *Ibid.*, 54-55.
14. Sharma, K.K., *Perspectives On Raja Rao—An article* (1980, Ghaziabad, Vimal Prakashan; Comrade Kirillov, An Appraisal by A.N. Gupta), 122-123.
15. *Ibid.*, 125.

16. Raja Rao, *Comrade Kirillov* (New Delhi, Orient Paperbacks, 1976), 53-54.
17. *Ibid.*, 35-36.
18. *Ibid.*, 56.
19. *Ibid.*, 46.
20. *Ibid.*, 83.
21. Mathur, O.P., *The East-West theme in Comrade Kirillov in New Literature Review*, Number 4, Special Indian issue, 27.
22. Raja Rao, *Comrade Kirillov* (New Delhi, Orient Paperbacks, 1976), 89.
23. *Ibid.*, 58.
24. *Ibid.*, 85-86.
25. Paranjapa Makarand, *The Best of Raja Rao* (New Delhi, Katha Classics, 1999), xiv.
26. Iyenger, K.R., Srinivasa, *Indian Writing In English* [Bombay, Asia Publishing House, 2002 (postscript), revised and enlarged edition], 739.

14

INFLUENCE OF *THE BHAGAVADGITA* IN ARUN JOSHI'S *THE FOREIGNER*

SIDDHARTHA SHARMA

Arun Joshi's *The Foreigner* (Hind Pocket Books, 1968) is deeply influenced by the *Bhagavadgita* as we discover Sindi Oberoi, the protagonist, quoting certain verses from it and trying to practice the principle of detachment preached therein. Actually the novel turns out to be Sindi's spiritual odyssey as the central message of the novel comes from the *Bhagavadgita*.

Sindi is demoniacal in nature. He is full of desire, does not believe in God or religion, lacks purity and good conduct and cannot make out the difference between the way of action or the way of renunciation. Deprived of parental love and affection in his very childhood, Sindi becomes broken and anchorless. He is full of passion and has sexual relations with Anna, Kathy, Christine and later with June. He wants to love June without possession. He dreads involvement and hides it in the garb of detachment. He does not believe in God. On being asked by June whether he believes in God, he shows his leanings towards the negative side. Even morality or immorality mean nothing to him. When Shiela says that June was not virtuous as she was not a virgin; he feels hurt and says, "It that all?" and further adds: "So you think one of these Marwari girls is really superior merely because of a silly membrane between her legs?" (60) He does not follow the norm of social conduct while talking to Shiela, an Indian girl leading a sheltered life. Lord Krishna tells Arjuna in the *Bhagavadgita*:

pravrttim ca nivrttim ca
jana na vidur asurah
na saucam na'pi ca caro
na satyam tesu vidyate. (Chapter XVI, Verse 7)

That is: "The demonic do not know about the way of action or the way of renunciation. Neither purity, nor good conduct, nor truth is found in them."[1] Further, the next verse says:

asatyam apratistham te
jagad ahur aniswaram
aparasparasanibhutam
kim anyat kamahaitukam. (Chapter XVI, Verse 8)

That is: "They say that the world is unreal, without a basis, without a Lord, not brought about in regular causal sequence, caused by desire, in short."[2]

Sindi believes that "there is no end to suffering, no end to the struggle between good and evil" (43). This is reminiscent of what Lord Krishna tells Arjuna:

yada-yada hi dharmasya
glanir bhavati bharata
abhyutthanam adharmasya
tada' tmanam srjamy aham. (Chapter IV, Verse 7)

That is: "Whenever there is a decline of righteousness and rise of unrighteousness, O Bharata (Arjuna), then I send forth (create incarnate) Myself."[3] And again in the next verse he says:

paritranaya sadhunam
vinasaya ca duskrtam
dharmasamsthapanarthaya
sambhavami yuge-yuge. (Chapter IV, Verse 8)

That is: "For the protection of the good, for the destruction of the wicked and for the establishment of righteousness, I come into being from age to age."[4]

The problems and bitter realities of life make Sindi seek refuge in non-involvement and inaction; but in the process he becomes the more pained. After Babu's death, June finds that she is pregnant by Babu, and asks Sindi to marry. The hypocrite and selfish Sindi, in the garb of detachment, refuses to marry her. She undergoes an abortion and dies. Sindi comes to a more sorrowful and repentant state. As Lord Krishna tells Arjuna:

duhkhan ity eva yat karma
kayaklesabhayat tyajet
sa krtva rajasam tyagam
nai krtva tyagaphklam labhet. (Chapter XVII, Verse 8)

That is: "He who gives up a duty because it is painful or from fear of physical suffering, performs only-the relinquishment of the 'passionate' kind and does not gain the reward of the relinquishment."[5]

He misconstrues the meaning of "detachment" which refers to the absence of desire detachment towards the world but to oneself as well. As Lord Krishna teaches Arjuna:

na karmanam anarambhan
naiskarnyam puruso' snute
na ca samnyasanad eva
siddhim samadhigacchati. (Chapter III, Verse 4)

That is: "Not by abstention from work does a man attain freedom from action, nor by mere renunciation does he attain to his perfection."[6]

In reality he is a hypocrite. He indulges his passions but dreads involvement. He talks of "illusion" and "detachment," but behaves like a selfish man all along. As the *Bhagavadgita* says:

karmendriyani samyamya
ya aste manasa smaran
indriyartham mimudhatma
mithyacarah sa ucyate. (Chapter III, Verse 6)

That is: "He who restrains his organs of action but continues in his mind to brood over the objects of sense, whose nature is deluded is said to be a hypocrite (a man of false conduct)."[7] Hence, like Arjuna, Sindi behaves in terms of "enlightened selfishness."[8] He is still ignorant and selfish and has learnt "only half the lesson" (192). The more he gets smitten by pain, the more he tries to detach himself, and the more he fails to relate himself meaningfully to the world.

His detachment receives a terrible jolt in his encounter with June Blyth, wherein he helplessly watches the crumbling edifice of his detachment and tries to resist it. He appears to believe in "*Brahma satyam jaganmithya*"—(God alone is truth the entire world is illusion). Once he told June that nothing ever seemed real to him, let alone permanent.

Sindi's attitude to life and love is in total disregard of the values of human relations, which leads to his obsession with non-involvement. When the moment of real involvement and commitment with June comes, it becomes "almost a countdown of my courage" (58). He knows "Love was like a debt that you had to return sooner or later. And if you didn't you felt very uncomfortable" (60). Herein lies the rub. As Asnani aptly puts it: "pleasure without involvement and love without possession are the values that condition the attitude and overall vision of Sindi."[9]

The small fortifications of detachment that Sindi had built around himself all his life are shattered to pieces when the redeeming episode of the crumbling of Khemka's business and the appalled spectacle of the "bundles of soggy humanity" (43). He identifies himself with them: "These are my people, I thought" (198). Khemka's arrest following Income Tax raid for swindling the Government gave him a god-sent opportunity to redeem himself. But Sindi, dreading involvement, refuses "to be dragged into the mess" (199). He believes that one must accept the responsibility of one's actions: "Mr. Khemka had to suffer for his own actions. In the past I had tried to put the consequences of my action on others, or presumed to take over their actions as my own. Both had boomeranged. In the end both had done more harm than good" (209). He tells Shiela: "Who are you and I to stand in the way? He must suffer if he wants to stop being a jackal and become humane" (217-18). These highlight the significance of the *Karmic* principle of the *Bhagavadgita* (no action of ours goes unrewarded or unpunished); "we reap what we sow."[10]

Sindi, not being totally devoid of emotions, could not maintain his non-chalance for long. Sindi happens to visit Muthu's one-roomed house in the slum where he lived with his tubercular wife and realises the "accumulated despair of their weary lives" (226).

Muthu, an illiterate labourer in comparison to Sindi Oberoi, a Ph.D. in mechanical engineering from the prestigious university of America, teaches him the distinction between detachment and involvement: "Sometimes detachment lies in actually getting involved. He spoke quietly, but his voice was firm with conviction" (225). Muthu becomes for him the most appropriate example of the ideal man—the man of steady wisdom. In the *Bhagavadgita,* Lord Krishna tells Arjuna:

duhkesu anudvigamanah
sukhesu vigatasprhah
vitaragabhaya krodhah
sttitadhir munir ucyate. (Chapter II, Verse 56)

That is: "He whose mind is untroubled in the midst of sorrows and is free from eager desire amid pleasures, he from whom passion, fear, and rage have passed away, he is called a sage of settled intelligence."[11]

He has learnt from experience that it is not action or escape but right action or involvement that turns out to be genuine detachment, the state of *'sthitaprajna'* of the *Bhagavadgita,* having the stability of mind and that 'yoga' and selfless action from alone can redeem man.

He becomes more or less a "*sthitaprajna*" abandoning attachment whatsoever as per Lord Krishna's preachings in the *Bhagavadgita*:

yagasthah kuru karmani
sangam tyaktva dhanamjaya
siddhyasiddhyoh samo bhutva
samatvam yoga ucyate. (Chapter II, Verse 48)

That is: "Fixed in yoga, do thy work, O winner of wealth (Arjuna), abandoning attachment, with an even mind in success and failure for evenness of mind is called Yoga."[12]

Sindi realizes that for him, "detachment consisted in getting involved with the world" (225). He decides to act in right earnest without any desire for "*lokasamgraham*" preservation or maintenance of the world), as Lord Krishna tells Arjuna:

lokasamgraham eva' pi
sampasyan kartum arhasi. (Chapter III, Verse 20, lines3-4)

That is: "Thou shouldst do works with a view to the maintenance of the world."[13]

Krishna's injunction to Arjuna is:

Karmany eva' dhikaras te
ma phalesu kadacana
ma karmaphalahetur bhrs
ma te saigo' stv akarmani. (Chapter II, Verse 47)

That is: "To action alone hast thou a right and never at all to the fruits; let not the fruits of action be thy motive; neither let there be in thee any attachment to inaction."[14] Dr. Susheel Kumar Sharma aptly remarks: "Sindi's fatal flaw is that he forgets duty but remembers detachment which for Lord Krishna is a vital necessity to do one's duty."[15]

Dr. S. Radhakrishnan explains the meaning of the term thus: "We have to act in the world as it is while doing our best to improve it. We should not be defiled by disgust even when we look at the worse that life can do to us, even when we are plunged in every wind of loss, bereavement and humiliation."[16] Towards the end Sindi becomes oriented towards duty without selfish desires; and says, "The fruit of it was really not my concern" (228).

Sindi becomes a man of action. He takes upon himself the crumbling Khemka's business empire for "there would perhaps be useful tasks to be done" (234) in future and thus he would have "a chance to redeem the past" (234).

Lord Krishna enjoins Arjuna:

Yad ahamkaram asritya
na yotsya iti manyase
mithyai' sa vyavasayas te
prapritis tvani niyoksyati. (Chapter XVIII, Verse 59)

That is: "If indulging in self conceit, thou thinkest 'I will not fight,' vain is this, thy resolve. Nature will compel thee."[17]

Thus, impelled by his intrinsic nature, Sindi's higher and enlightened self accepts involvement as the only sane option. He takes up the responsibility of steering Mr. Khemka's bankrupt business ashore. Thus, in *The Foreigner* we find a deep influence of the *Bhagavadgita* in the formulation and the resolution of the problem according to the *Karmic* principle propounded by Lord Krishna. As H.M. Prasad aptly observes: "The central message of the novel comes from the *Geeta.*"[18]

NOTES AND REFERENCES

1. S. Radhakrishnan, *The Bhagavadgita,* New Delhi: Harper Collins, 1996, 336.
2. *Ibid.*, 336.
3. *Ibid.*, 154.
4. *Ibid.*, 155.
5. *Ibid.*, 354.
6. *Ibid.*, 133.
7. *Ibid.*, 134.
8. *Ibid.*, 91.
9. Shyam M. Asnani, "Exploration of the Inner World: a Study of Arun Joshi's Fiction," *The Literary Half-Yearly,* Vol. xxx No. 2, July 1978, 99.
10. S. Radhakrishnan, *Indian Philosophy,* London: George Allen and Unwin, 1923, 244-45.
11. S. Radhakrishnan, *The Bhagavadgita, op. cit.*, 123.
12. *Ibid.*, 120.
13. *Ibid.*, 139.
14. *Ibid.*, 119.
15. Susheel Kumar Sharma, "Philosophical Reverberations in *The Foreigner,*" *The Novels of Arun Joshi,* edited by R.K. Dhawan. New Delhi: Prestige Books, 1992, 132.
16. S. Radhakrishnan, *The Bhagavadgita, op. cit.*, 69.
17. *Ibid.*, 373.
18. H.M. Prasad, *Arun Joshi,* New Delhi: Arnold Heinemann, 1985, 49.

15

THE PROBLEM OF INTER-RACIAL MARRIAGE IN TIMERI MURARI'S *THE MARRIAGE*

HEMLATA SINGH

The Marriage a novel written by Timeri N. Murari, was published in 1973. The novelist has here tried to explore the inter-personal relationships on two levels. First, the inter-racial marriage of Roger Thomson and Leela, Tekchand's daughter. Secondly, the cultural pulls and tensions which an Indian family settled in U.K. has to face.

The writer focusses our attention on the so-called encounter between East and West, not only at the level of people but also at the level of ideas. In the Indian context a marriage outside the caste, and community is not acceptable. Therefore, "Often the motivation of rebellion against the family comes from romantic love." Writes Meenakshi Mukherjee and points out that:

> R.K. Narayan maintains the theme of the eternal triangle, that perennial peg of Western story tellers to hang their novels upon, is useless for an Indian writer, our social condition not providing adequate facilities for such triangles (28).

Timeri Murari has utilized this triangle as he writes about the Indians settled in England. Hence, it is here that one notices the sharp antagonism and complementariness of Harbans and Roger, Premlal and Roger and Hari and Roger to each other; all sustained and activated by a care for boundary lines of racial demarcation and colour based distinctioin. They all belong to Indian community in England. Who are deadly against the inter-racial marriages. The problems of inter-racial marriage in *The Marriage* are grave and heart-rending and the consequences even more tragic and brutal.

Timeri Murari, a free-lance journanlist, divides his time between England and India and has a first hand knowledge of the Indian and the British culture. Hence, he has very keenly portrayed the problems which arise in the marriage between the two races, the white and the black.

The realistic description of the cultural and psychological problems make this novel fascinating and a poignant story of love, and marriage between two races. The whole scene is centered on the immigrant community of a small industrial town in England. The novelist moves from the circumference of life towards the core and portrays the magnetic pull towards the 'still centre.' His depths and heights in the inter-marriage problems, raise vital issues regarding social integration and the resistance from orthodoxy.

Tekchand was good though troublesome. 'But to having his daughter embracing a white boy.' This embrace of the white and black restores with the idea of imperial embrace, an embrace between Indian and Britain, which was an unusual phenomenon long back and was not accepted by either sides:

> The boy has a car, may be they do, all these people sleep with each other, Brothers, sisters, wives....They do it openly. They are so brazen. I see them in the pictures and on the streets (216).

It is here again that one notices the overall encounter in the novel between such fanatical and obsessed persons and the human world of interaction, inter-relationship represented in the painful experiences of Leela and Thomson Roger.

What happened between Leela and Roger is specifically described in terms of illegitimate sexual relationship by Harbans, who tells his friends:

> The girl has an Englishman and she embraced him before she left. She's cheap, that girl. Tell Tekchand about his prostitute daughter? He will really hit her (215).

Hari's and Prem Lal's contempt towards Roger, a white "loafer" reveals the feeling of an Indian youth's "Indianness" and their possessiveness, who revengefully is happy at the thought of the pretty girl being lashed for going against the ethical codes of the Indian community. On the other hand Roger was proud of Leela and it hurts him to hide her from his other white friends.

Leela and Roger became one in the darkness of passion and love:

> Leela had her eyes closed, her senses lay in her skin now (208).

They remain united physically and spiritually. She staked the honour and prestige of her family and society without a moment's hitch as she valued love more and had been involved with English approach towards love. Murari describes physical union to suggest their complete merger. There is no duality either at the spiritual or the physical level. He writes:

> Roger kissed her....his whispers soothed and eased her....sinking deeper....breaking the flesh and restriction of the past (209).

Nothing could be more in line with the ferment of cultural mutation than partially evolved with Indian sense and sensibility in marrying a boy of her parent's choice, cooking food for her husband, her lord, her swaami, and looking after children. But like a modern British girl she is more concerned with her own destiny than happiness keen for the desire of her parents. Her father holds:

> Leela had caused too much trouble only because she hadn't been married earlier. He should have arranged her marriage two years back. He had been a weak man. He had listened to the wishes of her daughter, he'd never let that happen again (284).

Yet a girl like Leela in her final gestures of becoming a part of the shocking situation points to possibilities of insight into the nature of such cultural diversity and unity:

> Her mother watched her from across the room. She divided her time between arranging Leela's jwellery and directing Leela what she should pack. If Leela, so much as touched a dress or a skirt, her mother frowned.... Her mother had made a sullen silence through her supervision (258).

Leela's father and mother are unable to understand and appreciate Leela's desire to belong to the British mode of living, its ethos and all its cultural nuances. Her parents are unable to understand the impact of the *socio-cultural milieu in Leela.* The novel presents this idea both in the lively encounter of people and in immobile symbols of immensity and diversity:

> How could you do this to me didn't I bring you up properly, Didn't I teach you how to behave, Didn't I see you how to be proper? Didn't I....the voice broke (285).

This stance between motion and stillness, silence and sound, sleep and awakening is the crystallization of the basic paradoxes in the novel. That a person like Leela has slipped out of her environment is a reflection on the timeless immensity of India that has been a shock for the others. She loved Roger to marry and settle. A part of author's total plan, communicated by images of inclusive immensity and breeding, in human and vegetative terms, which demolishes distinctions into something timelessly humane. Murari shows how racial intolerance, force have a way of passing into the individuals and situation into the ferment and compost heaps of racial antagonism. Thus, a victim of the racial violence Roger struggled for life:

> the blow on the back of his neck smashed his face, into the side of his car....his teeth bit deep into his lips, and stained the grey metal as he slid on to the ground (265).

The violence is not operating only on the mythical level but also on the social, and personal levels. Leela and Roger's private world of emotions lie totally shattered. The tragedy of Leela and Roger achieves a universal significance in the modern age.

Murari's treatment of marriage and love are against cultural synthesis. The sad fate of Roger, who lies in the hospital, whole body being bandaged, crying of pain and anguish. And Leela's tragic aspect, leaving for India is a comment on racial prejudices. Murari emphasizes the centrality of vision through the narrative symbolically that it is love not hate which can make the different races of the world live in peace and harmony.

WORKS CITED

Mukherji Meenakshi, *Twice Born Fiction.*

Murari Timeri, *The Marriage,* Mac Millan, India, 1973.

16

THE FICTIONAL WORLD OF RUSKIN BOND

MEENU S. SODHI

He is popularly acknowledged as one of the best short story writers for children. His forays into the field of essay-writing, vignettes, travel-writing, poetry, songs and love poems have met with success. As a novelist he has won much acclaim and recognition. His novels or novellas, as they are more popularly known, are limited in number as compared to his other writings. His first novel, *The Room on the Roof*, written when he was seventeen, received the 'John Llewellyn Rhys Memorial prize' in 1957. The other famous novels are *Vagrants in the Valley, Delhi is Not Far, The sensualist* and *A Flight of Pigeons, Love is a Sad Song. A Flight of Pigeons* has been made into a film by the name of *Junoon.*

Ruskin Bond was born in Kasauli in 1934, and grew up in Jamnagar, Dehra-Dun and Simla. As a young man he spent four years in the Channel Islands and London. He returned to India in 1955, and has never left the country since. His first novel *The Room on the Roof* received the John Llewellyn Rhys Prize, awarded to a commonwealth writer under thirty for a work of outstanding literary merit. He received a Sahitya Akademi Award in 1993, and the Padma Shri in 1999. He lives in Mussoorie with his adopted family.

His literary career began with *The Room on the Roof* in 1956. After a long lapse of time, in 1972 appeared, *An Axe for the Rani* this was closely followed by *Love is a Sad Song* in the year 1975. In the year 1980 appeared his novel based on the historical event of the Indian freedom struggle, the revolt of 1857. *A Flight of Pigeons* is classic novella about the twists of fate, history and the human heart. It was later adopted by a well known film maker and turned into a successful Hindi film by the name of *Junoon. Vagrants in the Valley* was published in 1981. *Delhi is Not Far* published in 1994.

In the course of a writing career spanning four decades, he has written over hundred short-stories, essays and novels and more than thirty books for children along with that he has edited three anthologies for Penguin Books. In 1995, Penguin Books published 'The complete stories and novels,' making him one of the ten authors to be so honoured. A 26-episode serial based on his short stories was also telecast by Doordarshan. In the year 1997, he wrote his first full-fledged memoir In *Scenes from a Writer's Life*, recounting his formative years. In his memoir along with his recollections we are rewarded by a lovely collection of photographs giving us a glimpse into the most important events, people and places in the eventful journey of our authors life. He writes:

> His first novel 'The Room on the Roof' first took shape in England, the land of his forefathers, where he was sent to make a career for himself in the field of writing. His first steps into this arena were marked by a lot of enthusiasm and high spirits. He writes about this phase in his 'memoir' that "...school behind me, I was all set to launch myself in the world as a writer. All glory comes from daring to begin!..." (*Scenes from a Writer's Life: A Memoir*, 78).

With such high spirits and high morals he finished writing his first novel in 1951. He mentions the fact in his memoir along with all the trials and tribulations that he had to go through, in order to see his first work in print. He writes, "1951 was to see the genesis of my first novel, and it was to shape my character for the rest of my days" (Scenes, 78). He further says:

> And what started out as a journal and then became a first person narrative finally ended up in the third person. But editors only made suggestions. They did not tamper with your language or style. And the 'feel' of the story—my love for India and my friends in particular was ever present, running through it like a vein of gold (Scenes, 78).

This remark gives us a deep insight into the personal feelings of a writer, still struggling for show-casing his talent to the world as well as a human being with deep and strong bonds of attachment to his friends, and a deep rooted love for India the country where he had been born, brought up and educated. His love for India has given birth to the Indian touch that we find in most of his writings and especially in his fiction. Mostly the setting of all his novels is Indian and maximum number of his characters are also Indians belonging to the different walks of life and also belonging to the different strata of society and at times to the various religions, that are to be found in this secular country. He has been very frank and open about his love and preference for India and generally all the things that are Indian. He remarks in *Memoirs* that— No sooner had I set foot in the west than I wanted to return to India and to all that I had known and loved (Scenes, xv).

He makes a reference to his divided loyalties as he was born into British India but ultimately his love for India won hands down and he very sincerely and truthfully confessed that "I had resolved most of my inner conflicts and could confidently say, 'I am an Indian' in the broadest all embracing, all Indian sense of the word" (Scenes, xvi).

And after this he made up his mind about his future which lay in this land, which he had adopted as his own— "This was where I belonged and this was where I would stay, come flood or fury" (Scenes, xv).

Once he made up his mind about the country and the place where he wanted to settle for his life, the second step of prolific writer came to him rather easily. The realization that he loved to write novellas instead of the traditional novels, also dawned upon him. The novella is shorter version of novel. Ruskin Bond's novels do not exceed hundred and fifty pages. His love for short stories seem to have a hand here, suggesting that he is not very comfortable writing lengthy narratives. A short story is meant to be read at one sitting. This fact is true about his novel as well. They must be finished in one sitting, otherwise the evanescent charm which characterizes them will disappear. The mood which is created in the beginning has to be maintained till the end because a certain mood is very important to read, enjoy and to appreciate his novels. He himself comments that—"Over the years I was to find that the short story or novella best suited my temperament: snatching at life and recording its impressions and sensation rather than trying to digest it whole" (Scenes, 75).

His love for short stories influences his method of presenting and writing his novels by pruning most of the unwanted details and by evoking the right kind of atmosphere and background. So his special love and susceptibility to children's literature influences the content of his novels. He confesses in his *Memoir*, that for his collection of material for his future writing, he found the company of children the most fulfilling and rewarding. He says, "And then I turned to children, probably because of their innate wisdom and thousands of years of civilization in their genes, but with all the freshness of a new life, a new day" (Scenes, 90).

Children occupy important and significant roles in most of his novels. The central-character of *The Room on the Roof* is a 17 year old Anglo-Indian boy by the name of Rusty, a teenager swinging between the extremes of childhood on one hand, and that of adulthood on the other. Rusty makes friends with many local boys of Dehra-Doon for Doon-valley is the setting of this novel. The entire novel evolves around these youngsters, the only adult of importance being Mrs. Kapoor with whom Rusty falls in love.

In the novel *An Axe for the Rani*, the most crucial and important character in murder mystery is Kamla, a girl of twelve or thirteen, around whom the whole mystery revolves and hers is a character that is shrouded in mystery and ultimately she is the one who holds the key to solving that murder mystery. The presence of Inspector Keemat Lal is very prominent throughout. Though he is middle-aged, yet he has some child-like traits and a basic innocence that generally we do not associate with grown-ups. He is quite unlike a police man in character. The friendship grows between Kamla and Keemat and little by little Kamla reveals to him the whole truth. It is the experience of most horrible kind that is faced by Kamla in this novel. She discloses to Keemat all about the Rani being a procuress for the wealthy businessman Dalip Singh. The Rani introduces the innocent and unsuspecting child Kamla to him. She is terrified by his advances and resists. Kamla reveals the truth about the whole mystery of murder, thereby solving the identity of the murderer.

Keemat Lal happens to learn a lot in this case and actually matures as a person and realises that law is not foolproof. Keemat Lal's career depends on his solving the case but his basic humanity, ethics and morality wins in the end. His final judgement is fair to the culprit and it is a victory of human values over the mundane considerations of promotion.

Ruskin Bond's world has an abundance of children or the world that he projects in his novels is a child's world. In *Love is a Sad Song* the narrator himself plays the leading part. He is nearly thirty years old and mentally just a teenager, a dreamer, an incurable romantic. He falls in love with Sushila, a school girl half his age, who in so many ways is wiser than him. Sushila has been depicted as a fifteen year old girl, who is very practical and mature in her out-look. She accepts in a very pragmatic way the man her family has chosen for her as husband and is perfectly resigned to her fate when they meet after the lapse of six years. He is surprised to find her so mature as to have reconciled to the compromise that her marriage was. Meanwhile the narrator has also grown-up and has matured ultimately to find and accept the truth that he has lost Sushila for good. When he leaves Shamli he does not seriously contemplate returning. Both characters have matured in their own way and in the different directions, one by getting married and the other by remaining unmarried.

A Flight of Pigeons is based on historical events. It is a totally different story set in Shahjanpur during the revolt of 1857. It is a haunting and beautiful love story, rich in its detail and historical facts. It is narrated in his simple and moving style, making a deep impact on the mind and heart of the reader. It again is a story of human passions and emotions, revolving around our main characters of Ruth Labadoor, who is the daughter of an English clerk working in British magistrate's office. She is a teenager of about thirteen only, just out of her school. She is caught in turmoil of conflicting emotions where her father is killed in an attack by sepoys, her family seeks refuge with their trusted family friend, Lala Ramjimal. From there they hope to escape to their relatives in Bareilly. But their plans are spoiled by the interference of Javed Khan, a fiery Pathan opposed to the British. He abducts Ruth and her mother and takes them to his haveli. They are terribly scared of the consequences, but to their surprise, it is not hate which has made him commit this act of abduction but almost a crippling passion for Ruth.

Ruskin Bond records in his *Memoir* about the personal touch that is to be found in the setting of this particular novel—

> The record shows that my father was born in Shahjahanpur, a small cantonment town which, coincidentally became the setting for my novella, *A Flight of Pigeons* (Scenes, 17).

The novelist explores the different inter-social relationship in the course of the narration with a touch of warm and penetrating observation. He brings out a very vivid picture of the society of Shahjahanpur at the time of the revolt. It traces the life of Ruth and her mother Miriam after their abduction by Javed Khan, who proposes marriage to Ruth. The mother of Ruth very intelligently and with great presence of mind handles the situation for almost a year, that they spend in his house. The combination of Javed's passion and impatience for Ruth creates a palpable tension throughout. The solution presents itself in the shape of the Fall of Delhi. With the restoration of British rule, Ruth and her mother escape to their relatives safe-keeping. At the end when Ruth thinks about the months they had been Javed's prisoners, she confesses her sneaking admiration for him. She also hopes for his safe escape from the hands of British Army.

Vagrants in the Valley is replete with personal touches. It traces the life of Rusty, an Anglo-Indian boy who in the company of his Indian friend Kishen, undertakes many adventures. The places described are Dehra-Doon, Rishikesh, Haridwar and the various hilly-villages, a favorite haunt of Bond. All his characters are Indian. He reveals his complete understanding and familiarity with all of them. The novel ends on the note of uncertainly as Rusty leaves India for Britain.

The novels are generally set in the hill station of Mussoori or the small but beautiful town of Dehra-Doon, with the exception of *A Flight of Pigeons* that has its setting in the busy and small town of Shahjahapur. The mention of Delhi is to be found in two of his novels, though the basic setting remains Mussoorie and Dehra-Dun But this was quite natural for him because he had spent most of his life in this part of the country. He was not familiar with other parts of the country to have described them with such ease and confidence. He is a lover of his surroundings. The natural wealth of plants and animals to be found in abundance in these parts of India. To him India was no ordinary country. It had a special importance and place in his life. According to him—"India is a atmosphere as much as it is a land" (Scenes, xv).

He is all praise for the lovely nature that is present all around him in India—"Mountains, valleys, fields and forests which had made an indelible impression on my mind" (Scenes, XV).

He even fell in love with not only the various sounds, melodies of different birds, animals and human beings but also with the dirt the filth and the heat and dust of India. They were quite soothing and lovely for him—"Every where noise and lights and smells; and smoke and dust; and filth and beauty. Oh India, my India for all your dust there is a blossom" (Scenes, 124).

He further recollects his thoughts and deep attachment with India, while he was away from the county he loved so passionately. He states that—"It was while I was living in Jersey in the channel Island that I really missed India" (Scenes, 131).

He realized to his utter amazement that—

> Even though I had grown up with a love for the English language and its literature, even though my forefathers were British, Britain was not really my place. I did not belong to the bright lights of Piccadily and Leicester square or for that, matter to the apple orchards of Kent or the strawberry fields of Berkshire. I belonged, very firmly, to peepal trees and mango groves; to sleepy little towns all over India; to hot sunshine, muddy canals, the pungent scent of marigolds; the hills of home; spicy odours, wet

> earth after summer rain, neem pods bursting; laughing brown faces; and the intimacy of human contact (Scenes, 154-55).

Human contact! That was what I missed most.... For in India there are no strangers... (Scenes, 155).

Till the time of almost three year that he had spent away from India, he grew more and more nostalgic about not only the lovely and familiar sounds and sights but also his friends, his acquaintances who had become an eternal part of his past and his memories. He could never find the warmth and intimacy of close relationship with the various other people that he met during his travel abroad. He constantly missed—

> The affection, the camaraderie, the easy-going pleasures of my Dehra friendships; the colour and atmosphere of India the feeling of belonging—these things I missed... (Scenes, 154). He adds, I had been away for over three years but the bonds were as strong as ever, the longing to return had never left me (Scenes, 155).

The personal elements are spread all over his writings and the novels are no different on that score. They have the visions and experience of a young boy, who had travelled the length and breadth of India, in the course of his childhood. The places that he made his home and the people that he befriended and came close to in the wake of his changing circumstances and the twists and turns of his young impressionable life and its thoughts. All these experiences, both bitter and sweet, find a mention throughout the world of his writing! The critics dismiss him as a writer of short stories, that too with a vein of personal touch running throughout, little realising the fact that childhood memories are the strong foundation of our adulthood. Ruskin Bond had rather very strong feeling about his memories and he refuses to let them go. The deep impact of his feelings, emotions and experiences can be seen, felt and read throughout his fiction or in other words in his novels, be it his natural beauty with its real sounds and sights or the stories with their life like vibrancy and the actual facts with some mingling of fiction to give them a life like aura and atmosphere, or for that matter, his characters who literally walk out of his personal life. All his Dehra-Dun friends find a place in his first novel *The Room on the Roof* and then in *The Vagrants in the Valley.* The central characters generally of all his novels are teenagers and youngsters because he confesses his partiality towards them and finds nothing very fascinating and appealing in the life of the grown-ups. According to him:

> To love and be loved is the greatest happiness...Men and women leave the age of childhood behind, and are so busy with their buying and selling, their ambitions and their hopes, their loves and their hates, that they forget they once lived in a land where dreams were real. I will not forget my childhood, I shall not surrender it (Scenes, 130).

Throughout his work of fiction, one thing that stands out very lucidly is his love of everything Indian. He might have been born to English parents but his love and attachment to the country of his birth is immense. Its lovely and dirty scenes as well as sites attract him and his deep-rooted emotional ties with his Indian friends is heart-touching. Through his writing he pays his homage to the country of his birth and he pays his tribute to the various friends, who made his life rich and complete.

WORKS CITED

Bond, Ruskin, *The Room on the Roof,* New Delhi: Penguin Books India (P) Ltd., 1993.

——. *A Season of Ghosts,* New Delhi: Penguin Books India (P) Ltd., 1999.

——. *A Flight of Pigeons*, New Delhi: Penguin Books India (P) Ltd., 2002.

——. *Vagrants in the Valley*, New Delhi: Penguin Books India (P) Ltd., 1994.

——. *Delhi is not Far,* New Delhi: Penguin Books India (P) Ltd., 1994.

——. *Scenes from a Writer's Life: A Memoir.* New Delhi: Penguin Books India (P) Ltd., 1997.

17

ANTITHETICAL PATTERNS IN UPAMANYU CHATTERJEE'S *ENGLISH, AUGUST*

MUKESH RANJAN VERMA

The full title of Upamanyu Chatterjee's maiden novel that was published in 1988 runs as *English, August: An Indian Story.* It is the antithesis between 'English' and 'Indian' that strikes the reader first, and this, in a way, also suggests the nature of the conflict in the novel. There are, however, several other antitheses in the novel that create patterns of meaning. It is the story of a metropolitan, upper middle class young man who has to undergo his training as an I.A.S. officer at a small provincial town. Agastya Sen, the son of a Governor, who has spent his life in two metropolises of India—Delhi and Calcutta—has so far been living an insular life centering around English literature, Western philosophy, music, soft drug and fantasies of women. Madna, where he has to have his training, is typical of the hundreds of small towns of India which have a sleepy look and a parochial outlook. The novelist hints at the incompatibility of these two worlds at the very beginning of the novel when Agastya is going from Delhi to Madna:

> Hundreds of kilometres of a familiar yet unknown landscape, seen countless times through train windows, but never experienced—his life till then had been profoundly urban. Shabby stations of small towns where the train didn't stop, the towns that looked nice from a train window, incurious patient eyes and weather beaten bicycles at a level crossing, muddy children and buffalo at a waterhole. To him, these places had been at best

> names out of newspapers, where floods and caste wars occurred, and entire Harijan families were murdered, where some prime minister took his helicopter just after a calamity, or just before the elections. Now he looked out at this remote world and felt a little unsure, he was going to spend months in a dot in this hinterland (4-5).

His apprehensions are confirmed at his very first encounter with Madna where he reaches at night. The small cigarette and paan shops lit by kerosene lamps, cattle and rickshaws jostling together on the road, overflowing drains, trucks splashing muddy water all around—he faces a world which he had never experienced. The government rest house where he has to stay during his probation has also nothing to put him at ease. Children of various sizes who all seemed to breathe through their mouths throng at the door of his room. The dinner is awful and the large number of mosquitoes, even though he sleeps under a mosquito net, give him a swollen face in the morning. All this gives him a feeling of unreality—"he felt as though he was living someone else's life" (5).

The day Agastya is to depart for Madna, his close friend, Dhrubo tells him, "I've a feeling, August you're going to get hazaar fucked in Madna" (1). This mongrel of Urdu and English, 'hazaar fucked,' aptly describes how he, in fact, does feel there. The problem with Agastya is that he cannot relate to Madna, not just the place but the kind of life he has to lead there. He is not a phony. Nor is he a ridiculous copy of the westernized Indian, some one like Mandy in the novel. The reason for his alienation in Madna lies in the fact that he belongs to that breed of urban Indians who find nothing in common with the rest of India. Kumar, the superintendent of police in Madna, tells him that he looks the 'English type.' When he expresses his surprise, Kumar says, "Any Indian who speaks English more fluently than he speaks any Indian language I call the English type." (23) When the Englishman, John Avery, visits Madna with his wife to see the obscure memorial of his grandfather who had been the district collector of Madna during the British days, the officials of Madna wait for August, who is away to Delhi, to take care of the couple. Thus people of Madna also look upon him as a class apart.

Upamanyu Chatterjee creates the antithesis between Agastya's past life and his present life at Madna by interspersing events from his boarding school days or his university days in Delhi or from his life in Calcutta with his activity at Madna. When he was at a boarding school in Darjeeling, he felt envious of the Anglo-Indian boys who spoke English with a different accent and who moved in the company of Tibetan girls:

> Agastya's envy had then blurted out, he wished he had been Anglo-Indian, that he had Keith or Alan for a name, that he spoke English with their accent. From that day his friends had more new names for him he became the school's' last Englishman' or just 'hey English' (his friends meant 'hey Anglo' but didn't dare) (2).

The nicknaming of 'August' from Agastya by his friends in Delhi, though nothing unusual among college boys, shows the kind, of metamorphosis that his persona underwent. Born in a traditional Bengali family he was given a traditional name from the Hindu mythology. Agastya, the sage who figures both in the Ramayana and the Mahabharata could, with his spiritual powers, push the mountain back. Agastya, his modern namesake, grows so lethargic after taking his daily dose of marijuana that he has no desire to exert his will one way or the other. The only occasion on which he does so is when as the B.D.O. of Jompana he visits the tribal area of Chipanthi which is hit by acute shortage of water. He forces the Deputy Engineer, Chaudhri and his subordinates, who have readymade official excuses for not doing their duty, to go and bring the tanker of water the same day to Chipanti. This strong reaction in him is partly the product of the moving sight of small children going, deep inside the lone dirty well of the village and bringing half bucketful of muddy water from there, in the process of which they are bruised, and partly the desire to make the callously irresponsible officials, to behave responsibly at least this once. About this act of August, Upamanyu chatterjee says in an interview:

> "The whole water issue is his first outward movement. But not in a dramatic way; it is just the hint of looking outward. Even though he is longing to be self-absorbed, events in themselves can pull a person out, yes I hope that was cautiously suggested though" (Prathima, 52-60).

Even this incident proves merely an occasional stir in the otherwise placid self-cocooned existence of Agastya at Madna where he responds to the people and activities around him with his outer self only, keeping his inner self-inviolate. That is why he fails to relate to Madna, even after a stay of nearly a year there.

In the character of Madhusudan Sen, Agastya's father, Upamanyu Chatterjee presents an antithesis to Agastya. Madhusudan Sen, a distinguished I.C.S. officer of the yester years, who had been Home Secretary and Chief Election Commissioner, is presently the Governor of West Bengal. With this spectacular career graph goes a rich personality. Agastya says about him to Sathe: "He's amazing, he eats corned beef sandwiches and wears dhotis and reads the Upanishads in Sanskrit" (281). About Agastya, the novelist tells us: "He had no devouring interests, and until he came to Madna, very little ambition" (4). Madhusudan Sen had anticipated the first reaction of Agastya to Madna and had told him that his job would give him glimpses of "other situations and existences which might initially prove startling" (94). So when he learns about his unhappiness in Madna, he is not surprised, but only a little saddened. He writes to him:

> But remember that Madna is not an alien place, you must give it time. I think you will like your job eventually, but if you don't, think concretely of what you want to do instead, and change (25).

In his second letter Madhusudan Sen tells Agastya about his own reaction when he had gone to the Konkan after joining the I.C.S.:

> Madna must have placed your Delhi and Calcutta in perspective, it must have. The same happened with me when I was in the Konkan, forty years ago. But I suppose my reactions were different from yours. After Presidency College, the Konkan was a wonderful surprise (149).

Agastya lacks his father's ability to respond to life's variety. He cannot look beyond the groove that he has created for himself. Despite his non-serious attitude towards most of the things, his flippant observations and glib remarks, he lacks the basic sense of humour to take the things in their right perspective, a sense of humour that teaches man that it takes all kinds to make the world, that living means taking life in all its spectrum. That is why Madna breeds a kind of frustration in him:

> Agastya was enraged at himself, for agreeing to the afternoon, for being in Madna, for a job that compelled him to be polite to Srivastav and his wife, for being in the job he was, for not having planned his life with intelligence, for having dared to believe that he was adaptable enough to any job and circumstance, for not knowing how to change either, for wasting a life (112).

Another character in the novel that creates an antithesis to Agastya is Baba Ramanna, the founder of Baba Ramanna Rehabilitation Home of Lepers in Madna. Agastya first hears of him when he comes to know that Baba Ramanna has refused the government help for his Home, not that he does not need it but because it would inevitably bring the government interference in the working of his Home which would only mean disaster for the Home. When a not so enthusiastic Agastya visits the Home, he is impressed by what he sees there. He does not meet the seventy seven year old Baba but his son, Raman Karanth, who takes him round the Home.

It is from him that he knows the story of the Baba. Shankaran Karanth, now popularly called Baba Ramanna, was a doctor who had a lucrative medical practice in Bangalore forty years ago. Like most of similar stories that have created legends, the story of Baba Ramanna's life is the story of the renunciation of Home for the realization of an ideal which in his case was the service of lepers, that section of humanity which was discarded even by the family and friends. Shankaran Karanth had realized that lepers needed not only medical help but also psychological help to restore their self-respect and self-confidence. This drew him to Madna, a place far away from Bangalore, but where land was cheap and the water table was high, and because of the famous temple at Gorapak there was a congregation of leapers there. His dedicated labour of all those years is now reflected in the cleanliness of the place, the organized life that the inmates of the Home lived and the self-confidence and zeal for life that they showed. Agastya's visit to the Rehabilitation Home leaves a deep but mixed impact on him:

> Initially, to him, Baba Ramanna had seemed pleasantly mad and completely remote, a do-gooder out of a book of legends for children, a small-time Ishwar Chandra Vidyasagar or a male Mother Teresa. Late in the evening, in unsettling flashes, Baba Ramanna's achievement had seemed inhuman, almost monstrous as Agastya stared at the fields and orchards, and the two wells, phoenixes that the Baba had helped to rise in triumph out of barrenness, he felt a little sick—at the immensity of a human ambition, but also at its nobility and virtue, at the limitlessness of the potential of human endeavour, but also the infinite patience and craft required to bring the endeavour to fruition (235-6).

Though Agastya talks of the limitlessness of the potential of human endeavour and realizes the importance of infinite patience in that endeavour, he himself shows no urge for it. He complains against almost every one in Madna. He seems disgruntled at everything. The work that he is supposed to learn does not interest him. One reason that he gives for it is that he does not understand the local language and so what transpires in different offices remains incomprehensible to him. He, however makes no effort to learn the language in all those months, despite Srivastav, the district collector suggesting him to do so at the very beginning of his stay at Madna. A.K. Singh's observation in this regard does not seem to be very convincing when he says:

> Chatterjee's protagonist does not relish this state of corruption, exploitation, indifference and snobbery, which aggravates his problems in Madna and makes him develop a strong aversion for this much coveted job. He tries to escape this crass culture as much as possible. In his insistent quest on (sic) uncompromising authenticity he sneers at Srivastav and Kumar and strips them off the official halo (96).

Nowhere in the novel does the protagonist show his aversion to corruption and exploitation, though he does make ironical comments on indifference and snobbery. If he walks out of the collector's revenue meeting, it is not out of protest but merely to escape boredom. In fact, he has been writing letters in that meeting. He never goes to office in the afternoon, but prefers to fantasize in his room at the guest house. If he really wanted to put an end to corruption and exploitation, he could easily have done so as the B.D.O. of Jompana where he had the entire official machinery at his disposal. Nor do we find in the novel any instance of his insistent quest for uncompromising authenticity that Mr. Singh refers to. In fact, though Agastya expresses his unhappiness in Madna, he himself is not very clear about what constitutes happiness for him. His concept of ideal life seems to be living in a metropolis, smoking marijuana, reading Marcus Aurelius, listening to music, either Western or Rabindra Sangeet and fantasizing about women. His uncle Paltukaku rebukes him for his, what he considers, irresponsible attitude towards life:

> And you want to leave the I.A.S., no less, after having been just a few months in the job. Disgusting. It would've been like your father wanting to leave the Indian Civil Service. For what? Not for a cause—Subhash Chandra Bose or somebody like that—but to be happy, you said this morning, all I want is to be happy. What you need is a whipping, I think your father is trying to be too reasonable. Sitting there at the Calcutta Raj Bhawan playing his silly games of patience, he attributes to you far more sense than you possess. You don't seem to like your place of posting because it is not Calcutta or Delhi, and it doesn't have fast food joints selling you hamburgers. You have always known security, that's why you're behaving so shallowly (161-62).

There is nothing wrong in a person's search for happiness, nor can his decision to give up his job be termed irresponsible merely because it is a coveted job. Many others have done so. But in their case they have generally been clear about their alternatives and preferences. In the case of Agastya this decision is governed by a negative—what he does not want. But it is not clear to him what he wants in its place. He thinks of joining Tonic's publishing firm, but, as Paltukaku tells him, he thinks of it only because it will give him a chance to live in Delhi. He knows nothing about publication, nor has he any interest in it.

In contrast to Agastya, his friend, Dhrubo is fed up with his job in Citibank. He is preparing for the I.A.S. examination. He is afraid that if he does not take the decision now, he might have to repent it at some later date. One person in the novel who knows what he wants in life and has chosen his path consciously and is happy about it is Govind Sathe, the cartoonist who is known as the joker of Madna. In this regard, he presents yet another antithesis to Agastya. Govind's father was outraged when he declared his decision to become a cartoonist, but he stuck to it. When Agastya meets him, he is an established cartoonist whose cartoons are published in four Marathi dailies, all published from Bombay and Pune. Agastya is surprised to hear this and asks him what he is doing in Madna. Govind's response is significant:

> 'Why, I like this place.' Sathe laughed and had to put down his cup because he couldn't restrain himself. With a question like that you really reveal yourself, Mr. Sen, your past, your bewilderment and boredom. Aren't you surprised at seeing me in Madna, I wear Levi's and read "Yes Minister?" (43-44).

Later in the novel, he tells Agastya that he could not live in a metropolis like Mumbai because there he felt lost. Madna for him is the home. For Agastya the search is still on. However, he is honest enough to realize that he could not remain in the I.A.S. merely because it was a coveted job and lent one a kind of social prestige. That is why, he decides to take a year off, like Drubo's American, to discover himself.

WORKS CITED

Chatterjee, Upamanyu, *English August*. New Delhi: Penguin Books, 1998.

Prathima, W.B., "Madna, Madras and Beyond: Upmanyu Chatterjee," *Literature Alive*. September, 1993.

Singh, A.K., "English August: An Indian Story: A Critical Appraisal," *Recent Indian Fiction*. Ed. R.S. Pathak. New Delhi: Prestige Books, 1994.

CONTRIBUTORS

Ashok Kumar Bachchan is Reader in English, Dept. of English, L.N. Mithila University, Darbhanga, Bihar.

Sarita Verma is Lecturer in English, B.D. Arya Girls' College, Jalandhar Cantt., Punjab.

P.S. Sanyal is Professor in the Dept. of English, C.M. College, Darbhanga, Bihar.

Pratibha Gupta is Lecturer in English, L.N. Mithila University, Darbhanga, Bihar.

Anita Parihar is the Head of the Dept. of English, Kumaun University, Nainital, Uttaranchal.

Ambuj Kumar Sharma is Reader in the Dept. of English, Gurukul Kangri University, Haridwar, Uttaranchal.

L.M. Joshi is Reader in English, Kumaun University, Nainital, Uttaranchal.

Manjusha Kaushik is Lecturer in English, Kanya Gurukul Mahavidyalaya, Haridwar, Uttaranchal.

Manju Roy is Lecturer in English, C.M. College, Darbhanga, Bihar.

H.P. Shukla is Reader in English, Kumaun University, Nainital, Uttaranchal.

Akhileshwar Thakur is Lecturer in English, T.N.B. College, Bhagalpur, Bihar.

Yogesh Kumar Sinha is Reader in English, C.C.S. University, Meerut, Uttar Pradesh.

Kavita Agrawal is a former Lecturer in English at Kanya Gurukul Mahavidyalaya, Haridwar, Uttaranchal.

Siddhartha Sharma is Lecturer in English, Mahatma Gandhi Gramodaya Vishwavidyalaya, Chitrakoot, Madhya Pradesh.

Hemlata Singh is Lecturer in English at T.P.S. College, Patna, Bihar.

Meenoo S. Sodhi is Lecturer in English at S.M.J.N. College, Hardwar, Uttaranchal.

Mukesh Ranjan Verma is Professor of English, Gurukul Kangri University, Haridwar, Uttaranchal.